Declaration of Peace for Indigenous Australians and Nature

Carved Law stick by Dr Tyson Yunkaporta.
'The stick tells the story of the Ouroboros (Serpent) on it, wrapped around the three-dimensional knob of the stick. The image is etched deep in the wood, with the tail not quite touching the mouth of the Serpent. Dingo and moon story of endless cycles of time is also carved alongside it. The stick is then rolled around the perimeter of a massive circle of clay, producing an image in relief of an endless line of creation serpents. Instead of an entropic enclosure under the second law of thermodynamics, this creates a closed loop of limitlessly regenerative energy and matter, shifting time into the first law of thermodynamics rather than the second'

Anne Poelina · Donna Bagnall · Mary Graham ·
Ross Timmulbar Williams · Tyson Yunkaporta ·
Chels Marshall · Shola Anthony Diop ·
Nadeem Samnakay · Michelle Maloney ·
Michael Davis

Declaration of Peace for Indigenous Australians and Nature

A Legal Pluralist Approach to First Laws and Earth Laws

Springer

Anne Poelina
Nulungu Research Institute
University of Notre Dame Australia
Broome, WA, Australia

Mary Graham
University of Queensland
Brisbane, QLD, Australia

Tyson Yunkaporta
Faculty of Arts and Education
Deakin University
Melbourne, VIC, Australia

Shola Anthony Diop
Sydney, NSW, Australia

Michelle Maloney
Australian Earth Laws Alliance
Narangba, QLD, Australia

Donna Bagnall
Curtin University
Perth, WA, Australia

Ross Timmulbar Williams
Brisbane, QLD, Australia

Chels Marshall
NIKIRI Institute
Deakin University
Melbourne, VIC, Australia

Nadeem Samnakay
Australian National University
Canberra, ACT, Australia

Michael Davis
Law School
The University of Sydney
Sydney, NSW, Australia

ISBN 978-981-99-9326-0 ISBN 978-981-99-9327-7 (eBook)
https://doi.org/10.1007/978-981-99-9327-7

This Springer imprint is published by the registered company Springer Nature Singapore Pte Ltd.
The registered company address is: 152 Beach Road, #21-01/04 Gateway East, Singapore 189721, Singapore

Paper in this product is recyclable.

Foreword

The latest report from the Intergovernmental Panel on Climate Change predicts grave consequences for human and non-human communities if dominant, Western societies do not change their relationships with the Earth.[1] The latest report by the Intergovernmental Science-Policy Platform on Biodiversity and Ecosystem Services predicts that more than one million species are imminently threatened with extinction.[2] This is 1000 times the background rate (if humans did not exist) and is predicted to rise to 10,000 times the background rate with current population growth, overconsumption and climate change.[3] According to the International Union for the Conservation of Nature, 41% of amphibian, 26% of mammal, 21% of reptile and 13% of bird species face extinction unless we reduce the human footprint upon the planet.[4] Experts warn that climate change exacerbates already grave human threats to biodiversity by raising temperatures, acidifying oceans, altering precipitation regimes, mistiming synchrony between plants and pollinators, thus rendering protected biodiversity no longer habitable, but leaving few places to which flora and fauna can migrate.[5] In other words, in many places, particularly in wealthy redoubts, humans have developed a deeply unhealthy relationship with the planet on which we depend.

[1] Intergovernmental Panel on Climate Change (IPCC), AR6 CLIMATE CHANGE 2021: THE PHYSICAL SCIENCE BASIS (2021), *available at* https://www.ipcc.ch/report/ar6/wg1/.

[2] IPBES, Media Release: Nature's Dangerous Decline 'Unprecedented'; Species Extinction Rates 'Accelerating.' *Available at* https://ipbes.net/news/Media-Release-Global-Assessment.

[3] Jurriaan M. De Vos et al., Estimating the Background Rate of Species Extinction. 29(2)CONS. BIO. 452 (2014). *Available at* https://doi.org/10.1111/cobi.12380.

[4] See https://www.iucnredlist.org.

[5] IPBES & IPCC, Biodiversity and Climate Change Workshop Report 15, 30. 2021. https://ipbes.net/sites/default/files/2021-06/20210609_workshop_report_embargo_3pm_CEST_10_june_0.pdf.

More than 10% of Australia's Land mammals have gone extinct since the 1850s.[6] In the 20 years between 2001 and 2021, Australia's tree cover decreased by 21%, emitting over 2 gigatons of carbon, which will further exacerbate global heating, and which will further destroy the nation's forests.[7] In 2019–2020, Australia was the world's leading exporter of metallurgical coal and the second largest exporter of thermal coal,[8] thus aggravating the planet's heating to levels that threaten continued life in the nation and elsewhere on Earth.

As the authors of this 'think tank of ideas' from Australia understand, it is not an accident that the savagery of how the dominant class has treated the planet is mirrored by the savagery of how that class has treated Aboriginal peoples. The ideology of domination links abuse of humans and of planet. Thus in this volume, Aboriginal and allied Australian thinkers convene to offer saner lifeways for planetary health. They offer rich testimonies that evoke what it means to see oneself as embedded in the landscape, to see one's life in relationship with the planet that sustains all life, including one's own.

Hegemonic legal thinking, as instantiated in Australia, has subjugated, and continues to subjugate Aboriginal peoples, while also subjugating the planet. Law itself needs healing if culture and nature, and nature-culture is to endure. As part of a program of reparations for the savagery the dominant culture has evinced, the authors assert that law must be decolonised. As Donna Bagnall expresses it below, they seek to 'Remedy the Australian Western law as it is sick and in decay'. The authors advocate for legal pluralism, for healing the dominant culture's law by infiltrating and intertwining that law with the autochthonous lore of the Land that has been the law of Aboriginal culture for tens of thousands of years.

This volume richly evokes what it means to live in an inextricable relationship with the Land. As Mary Graham notes, 'I am located, therefore I am'. Or, as Anne Poelina introduces herself in her story 'I am a Nyikina Woman who belongs to the Mardoowarra Fitzroy River'. When colonisers dispossessed people of their Lands, they also dispossessed them from their cultures, from their selves. Aboriginal law starts with First Law, asking people to adopt lifeways to the laws of nature, rather than hubristically thinking nature will respond to our legal prescriptions for it.

In *Dark Emu*, a bestselling volume that has evoked a paradigm shift in the way many Australians think about Aboriginal society, Bruce Pascoe writes that 'Human survival on a healthy planet is not a soft liberal pipe dream; it is sound global management and the deepest of religious impulses'.[9] The authors here look to co-design legal pluralism in Australia (and, by extension, elsewhere), where, as part of a decolonisation project, the Australian government incorporates Aboriginal law, founded in

---

[6] Adam Morton, Australia Confirms Extinction of 13 More Species, Including First Repitle Since Colonisation. *Guardian* 3 March 2021, *available at* https://www.theguardian.com/science/2021/mar/03/australia-confirms-extinction-of-13-more-species-including-first-reptile-since-colonisation.

[7] See https://www.globalforestwatch.org/dashboards/country/AUS/.

[8] Australian Government, Coal: https://www.ga.gov.au/digital-publication/aecr2021/coal.

[9] Pascoe, B. (2018). *Dark Emu: Aboriginal Australia and the birth of agriculture.* Magabala Books (p. 226).

co-management of Land according to Aboriginal principles of human/non-human co-relationship. The authors would reform the law to honour Aboriginal notions of interdependence by giving local communities authority to work with Lands according to their lore/law. Legal pluralism—particularly around alternate conceptions of nature to be instantiated in the law—is part of response and redress to colonial savagery.

This project has analysed some very tentative, tender buds in the nation. For example, it has looked at some recent groundbreaking developments in Western law that recognise Aboriginal connections with environments and ecologies. One such development is Victoria's *Yarra River Protection (Wilip-gin Birrarung murron) Act* 2017, which recognises the Yarra as 'one living, natural entity'.[10] The Act's Aboriginal title means 'keep the Birrarung alive'.[11] It is Australia's first piece of English/Aboriginal language legislation, and puts the relationship of Aboriginal peoples to the River at the centre of the Act. Wilip-gin Birrarung murron begins with Wurundjeri text, part of which reads, in translation: 'The Birrarung is alive, has a heart, a spirit and is part of our Dreaming. We have lived with and known the Birrarung since the beginning. We will always know the Birrarung … Since our beginning it has been known that we have an obligation to keep the Birrarung alive and healthy—for all generations to come'.[12] The Act notes the 'role of the traditional owners as custodians of the Yarra River Land' as well as the 'cultural diversity and heritage of post-European settlement communities'. That is, while the Act acknowledges the traditional owners, those communities will share responsibilities with the descendants of more recent arrivals.[13]

The Act creates an independent Birrarung Council, in a sense, 'the Voice of the River', which is appointed by the Environment Minister.[14] The Birrarung Council includes at least two Aboriginal traditional custodians, in addition to representatives from environmental groups, agricultural interests, and at least two 'skill-based' representatives (e.g. environmental planners) to speak for the River.[15] While the Council does not speak directly *as* the River, it is envisioned to advocate for the River's needs in a long-term planning process.[16]

Rethinking our relationship with the planet means reimagining governance of the human/non-human interrelationship. The *Yarra River Protection (Wilip-gin Birrarung murron)* Act gives just an inkling of what healing legal pluralism could look like in Australia. The authors of this volume look to combine the modern with the autochthonous, learning from each, all the while recognising that modern ecological science only reaffirms Aboriginal practice rooted in deep understandings of human/

---

[10] *Yarra River Protection (Wilip-gin Birrarung murron) Act, 2017* pt 1 s 1(a) (Austl.).

[11] *Id.* Preamble, at 1.

[12] *Id.* Preamble, at 1 (Austl.).

[13] *Id.* pt 2 s 12(2)-(3), at 13.

[14] *See id.* pt 5 s 48(1), at 36.

[15] *Id.* pt 5 s 48(1)(b), at 36.

[16] *Id.* pt 5 s 48(1) (Austl.).

nature interdependence, which modern 'resource management' too often ignores. Modern 'resource managers' often don't understand they are born into, and marinated in, a paradigm based in domination of, rather than interrelationships with, the natural world. One of the shining lights of this work is that it sheds light both from inside and outside the dominant culture on some of the unremarked features of that system of law. Law should come from the Land, not be imposed on the Land. When we see Land as creator of all life and remake law to respect that first principle, we set about healing nature and healing all cultures.

David Takacs
University of California Hastings
College of the Law
San Francisco, USA
takacsd@uclawsf.edu

Addendum to the Foreword

The central concern of relations between the two different laws in Australia—the Aboriginal traditional law of great age and the Western positivist law with its postulates rejecting morality in law—is the question of how to bring together different societies and legal systems with such different world views.

Aboriginal societies, with Custodial Ethics, ecological stewardship and Laws of Obligation, are built on a relationalist rather than a survivalist ethos. The monumentality of Aboriginal law resides not only in the old saying 'The Land is the Source of the Law'[1], and in its integrity, gravity and authentic majesty, but in its moral foundation all without the contradictions inherent in Western law.

Western law, in contrast, continues to be hierarchical, anthropocentric and enforced through the threat of state violence (survivalist rather than relationalist). John Austin (1790–1859) argued that law, as opposed to moral imperatives, should be viewed simply as a form of command, made by an acknowledged and legitimate ruler, that gains adherence solely by means of an effective punishment.[2]

So, a question that arises from the discussions in this book is: even if we were to resolve the contradictions in the legal systems, and the Land and the environment in general might be better looked after, with recognition in the common law of Indigenous laws, and with appropriate legislation, how could this be reconciled with the ongoing mistreatment of Aboriginal people in Australia? Today we still see that no one is ever held accountable for the many deaths in custody or prisons of Aboriginal people where even young children of 10–12 years old are still being put in jail; state authorities still break up Aboriginal families and Aboriginal people still suffer socio-economic disadvantage in mainstream Australian society.

The real task of improving and raising Western law to a higher ethical level where humane, respectful treatment of *Land and people*, becomes the norm, is obviously the real challenge. Furthermore, part of this task would be to also address the Aristotelian

---

[1] Black, C. (2010). *The Land is the source of the law: a dialogic encounter with indigenous jurisprudence*. Routledge, 2010.

[2] Austin, John. "The Province of Jurisprudence Determined" 1832. Encyclopedia.com 13 August 2013.

logic of the 'excluded middle' argument, which is so often utilised in the West's adversarial systems. It will be difficult but doesn't have to be a complete obstruction in making future law.

Hopefully, with respectful and courageous discussions about what law could come to mean, there could emerge in an organic way the embryonic form of an intact, collective spiritual identity for all Australians, which will inform and support our daily, safe lives, our legal and political systems, aspirations and creative genius.[3]

Mary Graham

December 2022

[3] Graham, M 1999, 'Some Thoughts about the Philosophical Underpinnings of Aboriginal Worldviews', *Worldviews Environment, Culture, Religion,* 3.

Declaration

I declare my story titled *Narratives of First Law from the Martuwarra Fitzroy River* consisting of 12 pages in length, which is less than 10% of the full manuscript 124 pages as submitted herewith, titled *Declaration of Peace for Indigenous Australians and Nature: A Legal Pluralist Approach to First Laws and Earth Laws* (Poelina, A., Bagnall, D., Graham, M., Williams, R., Yunkaporta, T., Marshall, C.,Diop, S., Samnakay, N., Maloney, M. and Davis, M.), was developed into a 22-page publication and submitted as a separate peer review publication titled '*Ancient Wisdom Dreaming a Climate Chance*', authors Martuwarra RiverOfLife, Poelina, A., & Perdrisat, M. (In Review). Editors: Penteado, A., Chakrabarty, SP. and Shaikh, OH. (2023). *Traditional Knowledge and Climate Change: An Environmental Impact on Landscape and Communities*, Springer: Singapore. (unpublished)

I make this declaration in good faith, to have full disclosure to resolve any conflict of copyright and request this story be left as written within this manuscript as it has been referred to by other authors of the manuscript.

I make this Declaration on 19 October 2023.

Prof. Anne Poelina

Acknowledgements

This book has benefited from collaborations and the collective wisdom and lived experiences of colonialism witnessed through Indigenous people's stories—from the past, in the present and dreaming of a new and just future.

In partnership with non-Indigenous colleagues, we have written a book which we believe informs current legal practice. The Think Tank, literature reviews and analysis in the book are all informed by insights gained from diverse legal practitioners. We acknowledge the active participation of the Indigenous storytellers, all championing the need to shift from 'wrong to rights, justice and equity' for the generations of our families of past, present and into the future; Mary Graham, Anne Poelina, Chels Marshall, Donna Bagnall, Ross Williams, Tyson Yunkaporta and Shola Diop provided rich insights that have shaped this book. Individually and collectively, these Indigenous leaders share their personal reflections on how Australian law fails to uphold the holistic principles espoused by First Law and Earth-centred law, and they suggest alternative legal futures. These stories are presented as case studies, and through collective wisdom, with much talking, writing, reviewing and more talking and writing with our non-Indigenous colleagues, we present this book in a spirit of good faith and goodwill. We send the Dream out as a '***Declaration of Peace for Indigenous Australians and Nature: A Legal Pluralist Approach to First Laws and Earth Laws***'.

Contents

List of Figures

Chapter 1
Introduction

1.1 Purpose of This Book

As the world enters a time of multiple ecological and social crises—with climate change, biodiversity loss, ecosystem decline and the escalating gap between rich and poor communities affecting us all—there is a growing awareness that we can't respond to the challenges we face, with the same governance systems that brought us here.

In this book, we propose that the Western legal system has played a key role in supporting the extractivism and exploitation of people and nature that has brought us to where we are today.

In Australia, the Western colonial legal system is not fit for purpose and we must look to different laws and governance, if we are to reshape society so that human communities and the living world we depend on, are to have a healthy future.

The legal systems created millennia ago by the First Nations Peoples of the continent now known as Australia offer wisdom and governance approaches that are much needed at this time. Indigenous peoples' knowledge, culture and law are not just important to their own lives and livelihoods—they are also critically important to the long-term health and wellbeing of people in our region, and around the world.

We argue that Australian society needs to rethink its foundations and its future, and will benefit from Indigenous wisdom if it can appropriately acknowledge and connect with Indigenous First Laws. This book explores a number of ways that Western law in Australia can connect with Indigenous First Laws.

The book begins with a critique of Western law in Australia and the way it frames and treats Indigenous peoples and nature. It then shares stories from Indigenous perspectives about what First Laws are, and why they are vital to our future. It discusses several different ways that Western law can begin to respect and connect

---

The original version of the chapter has been revised. A correction to this chapter can be found at https://doi.org/10.1007/978-981-99-9327-7_6

A. Poelina et al., *Declaration of Peace for Indigenous Australians and Nature*,
https://doi.org/10.1007/978-981-99-9327-7_1

with First Laws, and offers some suggestions about how Indigenous peoples think we can influence legal pluralism in our nation to ensure everyone is equal under the law. Only then can the nation properly act and work to support Indigenous peoples' laws and culture and protect the environment.

As stated by Fernandez-Llamazares:

> Supporting Indigenous Peoples and local communities to secure and strengthen collective systems of tenure, governance, and ways of life is one of the most powerful ways to safeguard ecosystems from intensive and/or unnecessary development and to maintain the biocultural integrity of the territories in which Indigenous and Local Knowledge (ILK) is embedded …
>
> The cumulative, diverse, interacting, and pervasive pressures of the colonial and globalized post-colonial world continue to drive the loss of ILK systems worldwide, despite their resilience and adaptability. Such threats can only be addressed effectively through urgent and concerted efforts that foster transformative change, tackling deep structural interventions, systemic barriers, and leverage points in the current systems of decision making.[1]

It is the purpose of this book, consistent with Fernandez-Llamazares' comments, to make the case for a more just, interconnected, and healthier planet, linking Indigenous peoples' deep knowledges, histories and Laws, and ecologies, to those of others, and with other, non-human species.

1.2 Approach Used in This Book

1.2.1 Indigenous Think Tank

This book has been led and prepared by an Indigenous cultural team, an Indigenous 'Think Tank' with collaboration from non-indigenous lawyers and writers, to provide insights about what Indigenous people think about the current legal system and what Indigenous people believe should happen to strengthen protection for Indigenous people and the environment.

In addition to providing the insightful and moving stories in Chap. 3, Personal Stories, the members of the expert Indigenous cultural team have reviewed draft versions of this book and have assisted in its finalisation. Three online workshops were held to coordinate the stories and to share insights and ideas. The Indigenous team included Professor Anne Poelina, who convened and chaired the workshops, Mary Graham, Ross Williams, Dr. Chels Marshall, Shola Diop, Dr. Tyson Yunkaporta and Donna Bagnall. Our non-Indigenous team comprises Dr. Michelle Maloney, Dr. Michael Davis and Dr. Nadeem Samnakay.

[1] Fernandez-Llamazares, in Reyes-Garcia et al. (2019).

1.2.2 *Different Approaches for Australia and for the Pacific*

The First Laws of Indigenous Peoples in Australia are ancient; they have emerged from the deep relationships that the First Peoples have with the living world, and they continue to guide Indigenous culture, ethics and practice.

The laws and culture of the Peoples of the Pacific are also unique to the peoples and places from where they have emerged. They have been woven through the relationships people have with the land, sea, spirituality and with each other for centuries. Given these connections, it is vital that the First Peoples of the continent now known as Australia have a key role in co-designing legal pluralism, to ensure human, multiple species and environmental justice and equity. Peoples brought to Australia from the Pacific by the colonial governments should also have a role in influencing future law in Australia.

1.2.3 *The Power of Personal Stories*

A vitally important part of this book is Chap. 3, which shares personal stories and perspectives from the members of the Indigenous Think Tank: Mary Graham, Anne Poelina, Tyson Yunkaporta, Chels Marshall, Ross Williams, Shola Diop and Donna Bagnall.

The stories combine personal reflection, accounts of lived experience and legal analysis. They are guided by the following questions:

1. What is your lived experience, knowledge and or practice of First law (customary law or traditional law)?
2. How can this wisdom of First law influence legal pluralism?
3. How can the Indigenous philosophy and First Law principles help create legal and institutional systems which give effect to peace with nature and with Indigenous peoples?

Mary Graham begins this exploration by outlining the deep physical and philosophical connection that Aboriginal people have to Country. She does this by emphasising that it is the Land that sets Laws, therein placing obligations on humans, and in so doing manifest in cultural connections and identity based on Place, which she eloquently states as ‘I am located, therefore I am’. Colonial law and its preferencing of survivalism (win at all costs) are anathema to Aboriginal peoples’ Law and their connections to Land. This serves to emphasise that colonial law, if not accompanied by legal pluralism, will in certain circumstances continue to entrench harm on First Nations people and Country.

Professor Anne Poelina then provides a number of vignettes from community Elders and noted researchers who ground the broader philosophies introduced by Mary. This is done by drawing upon the knowledge and views of collective wisdom from people associated with the Mardoowarra/Martuwarra[2] River in the Kimberley region of Western Australia. The RiverOfLife, as it is also referred to in peer-reviewed literature, presents a way to anchor the intrinsic connections between Land, water and livelihoods as connected entities which, in the main, is not how colonial laws and governance systems view social ecological systems. This is exemplified by legislation in relation to water, or Land, or social and economic components. Anne Poelina concludes this narrative by offering the gift of ancient traditional wisdom as a way of navigating through our current predicament of climate change and the disconnect of growth at the expense of ecological limits. She emphasises that sustainable development is different from sustainable lifeways; the former being dominated by the paradigm of continuous growth—which cannot be sustained.

Ross Williams, Dr. Chels Marshall and Dr. Tyson Yunkaporta then, respectively, present their personal stories of connection to Country, revealing their experiences growing up as children and learning about the Land from Elders. Ross provides a rich explanation of how his early experiences with Elders taught him about nature, culture and Indigenous science. Chels also follows this theme but similarly concludes as Anne does that Indigenous knowledge offers a deeper granularity of understanding cause-effect relationships (such as that seen in seasonal calendars) and which can help observe, monitor and address environmental change and especially climate change. Tyson draws upon the science of physics to communicate the differences between colonial use of resources as closed systems and the impacts this has on the environment (Country), juxtaposed against First Law principles which are more cognisant of cause-effect relationships and feedback loops.

Each author ends in a solemn conclusion of loss of identity, culture and belonging and even a loss of hope if things do not change. Their reflections highlight that in their lifetime alone (a single generation), the values they hold precious have rapidly deteriorated through destruction of the environment. These stories collectively offer a sobering tale of dispossession and marginalisation, highlighting that urgent transformative change is required, drawing upon Indigenous knowledge and practice.

The pain of dispossession and marginalisation is acutely brought home by Shola Diop who recounts the forced repatriation of South Sea Islanders to mainland Australia in what was indisputably slavery. Shola recounts the additional trauma on Islanders when ‘indentured labourers’ were then forcibly returned to their Island homes, only to be ostracised upon their return. This resulted in hybridisations of custom, which still strongly unite South Sea Islanders through *Wantok* kinship systems. Shola concludes by emphasising that this customary-based unity has most noticeably united Melanesian’s in their advocacy for climate change and environmental justice.

To conclude on a positive note, Donna Bagnall reviews some key legal cases, and highlights where we can draw upon existing colonial law to help enforce First Law rights. She presents compelling legal precedents which can be used as leverage

[2] Mardoowarra/Martuwarra are used as alternative spellings from different Kimberley Aboriginal languages.

points for enforcing First Nations customary rights, in the main through existing Native Title law. Donna's review, while still advocating strongly for institutionalising legal pluralism in Australia, identifies strategic and practically applicable actions to consider in order to integrate Indigenous knowledge into Western law, advocate for Earth Laws to support First Laws and recognise Indigenous sovereignty.

Reference

Reyes-Garcia, et al. (2019). The contributions of indigenous peoples and local communities to ecological restoration. *Restoration Ecology, 27*(1), 8.

Chapter 2
Reflecting on Australia's Current Legal System

2.1 What's Wrong with Australia's Legal System?

2.1.1 Western Law in Australia is Sick and in Decay

In the dominant Western system, the 'Rule of Law' is arguably on the brink of entering a death spiral due to the numerous corruptive and corrosive factors that are prevailing in the system. The Australian legal system's structural integrity is under attack and as a result, it has been dislocated and is at risk of tumbling over.

Aunty Mary Graham has aptly described Western law as 'half law' and First Law as 'full law'[1] in terms of achieving a sustainable life and fulfilling the obligation to protect our common environmental treasures and their essential life support systems for all. This is very true as the Australian Western law has many flaws and, in many fundamental ways, the Western law will never be First Law because First Law is the 'Law of the Land', not the 'law of humankind'. As Professor Anne Poelina has also observed, Western law is about the 'me' (individuals), whereas First Law is about the 'we' (the collective).[2]

However, in addition to this, the Australian legal system is a pale and poorly version of itself, so it does not even recognise itself anymore. At the moment, therefore, it could be said that the Western law is more like 'quarter law' because of its dilapidated condition.

The extent of the decay is well illustrated by the 'Sports Rorts' pork-barrelling scandal under the Morrison government. 'Pork-barrelling' is the exercise of ministerial discretion in the making of grants of public money to community groups, especially in marginal seats, in the period prior to an election. The Australian National Audit Office (ANAO) review subsequently concluded that Minister McKenzie had

[1] Mary Graham in Yunkaporta and Kelleher (2021).

[2] Dr. Anne Poelina, Ibid.

A. Poelina et al., *Declaration of Peace for Indigenous Australians and Nature*,
https://doi.org/10.1007/978-981-99-9327-7_2

no legal authority to award the grants, totalling $100 million, to the allocated recipients.[3] The 'Rule of Law' is currently in a patent state of decline and decay, and this view is affirmed by preeminent constitutional law Professor Anne Twomey.[4] Twomey characterises this as a preference for 'constitutional risk' over strict compliance with the rule of law. This is an indictment on the Australian government, who should be a model citizen in upholding the law.

Another instance calling into question Australia's lawfulness and conscience was the long-term detention of the Tamil asylum seeker family from Biloela, the Murugappans, including their two children born in Australia, who were held indefinitely on Christmas Island by the Australian government. It was of such dire moral concern that former High Court Chief Justice Sir Gerard Brennan felt compelled to publish an op-ed and weigh into it., Sir Brennan described it as:

> (...) unconscionable to impose deliberate cruelty on those children to rectify the earlier failure to exclude the parents. … It would be a cruelty obnoxious to Australian values to deprive those children of their parents and it is cruelty obnoxious to Australian values to isolate them with their parents to discourage future people smugglers. Basic and important Australian values are at stake. They must not be discarded by a show of heartlessness towards Australian children.[5]

Prominent environmental cases in point include the Federal Court decision in the high-profile *Adani* water trigger case (2021)[6] in which the Australian Conservation Foundation (ACF) successfully established that then Environment Minister Sussan Ley had failed to duly apply the water trigger to assess the Adani coal mine's water pipeline under the *Environment Protection and Biodiversity Conservation Act 1999* (EPBCA), and accordingly, the proposal for the water infrastructure for the coal mine was unlawfully approved by the Federal government.[7]

The Federal Court held that ACF's interpretation of the water trigger provisions should be accepted and the Minister's rejected. A proposed action will constitute part of a 'large coal mining development' for the purposes of the water trigger controlling provisions 'if the action is so closely associated with the mining of coal as to be integral to it'.[8] As the proposed pipeline was integral to the mining activity, being the alternative water supply for the Carmichael coal mine, the proposed water infrastructure was part of the 'coal mining activity', and required the Commonwealth to consider whether the water trigger applied. The Court held the Minister's delegate had committed an error of law, and as a result, the controlled action decision was set aside and remitted to Minister for determination according to law.

---

[3] Australian National Audit Office (ANAO) (2020). See Conclusion, point 8. "…it is not evident to the ANAO what the legal authority was". Available at: https://www.anao.gov.au/work/performance-audit/award-funding-under-the-community-sport-infrastructure-program.

[4] Twomey (2021). Available at: https://www.cjccl.ca/wp-content/uploads/2021/05/10-Twomey.pdf

[5] Brennan (2021).

[6] *Australian Conservation Foundation Incorporated v Minister for the Environment* [2021] FCA 550, per Perry J.

[7] Australian Conservation Foundation (ACF) (2021).

[8] Ibid., [11–12] and [104].

Another more recent illustration of the gravity of the problem is the landmark case of *Waratah Coal v Youth Verdict* (2022)[9] in which the Land Court of Queensland (LCQ) found that several human rights would be limited/infringed by the Waratah coal mine, for which the Queensland government was considering issuing an environmental approval and a mining lease. In relation to climate change, her Honour found that the following rights of certain groups of people in Queensland would be limited: the right to life, the cultural rights of First Nations peoples, the rights of children, the right to property and to privacy and home and the right to enjoy human rights equally [44].

The LCQ duly applied the principles of ecologically sustainable development (ESD) in deciding what recommendation to make. Applying this approach, President Kingham stated that the precautionary principle meant that the decision-maker was required to take a cautious approach to the application given the uncertainties about the impacts on the Bimblebox nature refuge and about which climate outcome is realised in the future. In addition, her Honour found that approving the application "would risk disproportionate burdens for future generations, which did not give effect to the goal of intergenerational equity, and there were also intragenerational inequities in the way in which climate change impacts are experienced between different groups of people in Queensland." [1938].

The Court rejected Waratah Coal's argument that the relationship between approving the mine and climate change was too remote, indirect and not specific to this mine. Her Honour found that the relationship between emissions and temperature increases established by the climate science was linear, and the connection between the mine and climate change was sufficient to constitute a limit to human rights, and that this limitation was not demonstrably justified, in breach of the *Human Rights Act 2019* (Qld) [29–44].

In her Objection decision, President Kingham held that the importance of preserving the human rights, given the nature and extent of the limitation to the rights, weighed more heavily in the balance than the economic benefits of the mine and the benefit of contributing to energy security for Southeast Asia. Therefore, the Court ruled that her recommendation was Queensland government should refuse the planning approval and the mining lease on these grounds.

There are countless further examples that could be cited. As Professor Twomey points out:

> (…) when the rule of law is disregarded because it is inconvenient, when governments calculate how they should behave according to what they can get away with, when public servants facilitate such action rather than insisting upon the application of the law, and when power is seen as giving immunity from the application of rules and impunity from the legal consequences, then the rot in the democratic system has begun and will spread unless action is taken to stop it.[10]

---

[9] *Waratah Coal Pty Ltd v Youth Verdict Ltd & Ors (No. 6)* [2022] QLC 21, per President Kingham.
[10] Twomey, op. cit., p. 341.

In addition, the fundamental body of law known as equity is being overlooked and ignored to a large extent in our legal system. The common law is dominating and discriminating, and equity is in short supply for Indigenous peoples.

Therefore, Australia's Western law needs some major remedial adjustments in order to be moved sideways, back towards its true location, and closer to First Law so that the two systems are co-located in their relational proximity to one another.

We need the Australian Western law to resemble its true self again so that it can walk in peace together with First Law and in harmony with Indigenous ethics, in a consistent but truly plural system which allows the differences to shine through and to add value, without harming our shared wellbeing and futures—see Fig. 2.2.

Instead, at present, the Australian Western law is unlawfully dominating, in all of the ways discussed further below. The transformation proposed in this book would fulfil our nation's destiny to implement a plural Australian legal system. We use the word *destiny* because it is one that we technically already have under the Australian common law, but which is not being given full effect in our law.

2.2 Western Law in Australia Fails to Properly Recognise Pre-existing Indigenous Law

In legal terms, Australia today is a Federation, made up of three tiers of government: a Federal or Australian government created by the *Constitution of Australia 1901* (UK); State and Territory governments which evolved out of the original colonies founded by the British Empire and local Councils, which are the creation of State Parliaments.

Since the British Empire claimed the continent now known as Australia, the First Peoples of this continent have been treated with cultural ignorance, institutional racism and the horrors of genocide. The ancient pre-existing legal and governance systems of the First Peoples of Australia were not recognised by the British Empire nor the post-1901 Australian government. In 1992, the *Mabo* case[11] finally saw legal recognition of the First Peoples' prior and existing claim to their homes and estates. The *Mabo* case began a process of recognising Native Title but is a contentious and flawed approach to recognising the legal system that existed prior to colonisation.[12]

The reasons why First Peoples in Australia were treated the way they were, by the colonisers and successive governments, is shameful and a topic of much discussion and debate. At the time the British claimed/invaded the continent, so-called international law (law made by European powers for European powers, to support their

[11] *Mabo v Queensland* (No. 2) (1992) 175 CLR 1.

[12] For a discussion about the limitations of Native Title in Australia, see Irene Watson, 'Sovereign Spaces, Caring for Country and the Homeless Position of Aboriginal Peoples' (2009) 108(1) *South Atlantic Quarterly* 27 and also Irene Watson, 'Aboriginal Laws of the Land: Surviving Fracking, Golf Courses and Drains Among Other Extractive Industries' in Nicole Rogers and Michelle Maloney (eds), *Law as if Earth Really Mattered: The Wild Law Judgments Project* (Routledge, 2017) 215.

colonisation of non-European Peoples and places) identified three different ways that new lands or colonies could be claimed. Lands could be settled, conquered or ceded.[13]

By claiming that the continent was 'settled' (not conquered), it meant that the British government treated Australia as a colony that was uninhabited by a recognised sovereign or by a people with recognisable institutions and laws—'terra nullius', or empty Land. There were no treaties created with any First Peoples and no legal recognition or arrangements made for proper relations. British law—and institutionalised racism and genocide—was simply imposed on the original inhabitants. So today, while Indigenous people continue to respect and practice their ancient First Laws,[14] the ongoing colonial legacy of the British and now Australian legal system means these laws are largely ignored or disrespected by Australian law, except in relation to the flawed construct of Native Title and other colonial cultural heritage style laws.

2.3 Western Law in Australia Has Failed to Care for Our Environment and Heritage

Another challenge for Australian law—currently operating within the Western legal structure—is to fundamentally rethink and re-conceptualise the foundations of legal approaches to heritage, environment and 'resources'. This includes interrogating the kinds of discourses and narratives used to frame heritage, environment and resource protection.

From the time of colonisation to the present, the dominant world view and discourse in state centred governance and legal policy has been economic growth, extractivism and expansionism. In the present system, where environment and heritage are deemed to be under threat, or at risk of desecration, despoliation or destruction, the emphasis is largely on court-based litigation processes to prevent imminent harm. If the concept of 'heritage', and the management and governance of heritage, is interrogated, to critique and 'de-centre' its underpinnings within a predominantly Western Eurocentric framework, then it becomes possible to envisage

[13] Justice Blackburn in *Milirrpum v Nabalco Pty Ltd* (1971) 17 FLR 141, at 201, articulated the distinction thus:

> There is a distinction between settled colonies, where the land, being desert and uncultivated, is claimed by right of occupancy, and conquered or ceded colonies. The words 'desert and uncultivated' are Blackstone's own; they have always been taken to include territory in which live uncivilized inhabitants in a primitive state of society. The difference between the laws of the two kinds of colony is that in those of the former kind all the English laws which are applicable to the colony are immediately in force there upon its foundation. In those of the latter kind, the colony already having law of its own, that law remains in force until altered.

[14] See, e.g., Poelina et al. (No. 3).

spaces for strengthening and privileging Indigenous legal systems within more plural and polycentric formations.

There is a body of literature that sits broadly within a decolonising or anti-colonial framework, which examines alternative epistemologies, philosophies and concepts around heritage. This body of literature includes discussions of the diverse approaches to Indigenous heritage and law. One of the key themes that arises from readings of this literature calls attention to the 'holistic' nature of Indigenous peoples' cultures and societies. In this frame, 'law' is not seen as a discrete entity or discipline, but, instead, is intricately interconnected with all aspects of peoples' lives. As is shown in other places in this review, Indigenous Law encompasses a wide range of dimensions, including, critically, Indigenous knowledges and epistemologies. A powerful critique of Eurocentric knowledge systems, epitomised by what is generalised as 'Western scientific' knowledge, is presented by Santos, for example. Advocating a decolonising frame, Santos calls for a fundamental shift in the ways in which we think epistemologically:

> Colonial domination, oppression, and the relations between the colonizer and the colonized became key to my understanding of the various forms of domination, because forms of domination never act as pure forms but rather in a constellation of oppressions. That is why my thinking has increasingly turned to epistemological issues – that is, an engagement with the ways of knowing from the perspectives of those who have systematically suffered the injustices, dominations and oppressions caused by colonialism, capitalism, and patriarchy. This is the definition I give of 'epistemologies of the South': a crucial epistemological transformation is required in order to reinvent social emancipation on a global scale. These evoke plural forms of emancipation not simply based on a Western understanding of the world.[15]

Privileging of 'Authorised' Heritage and Environment Discourses

In some of the critiques of dominant Western, or Eurocentric heritage discourses, Waterton and Smith, among others, have identified what they have termed a Western 'Authorised Heritage Discourse' (AHD), which is 'a professional discourse that validates and defines what is or is not heritage and frames and constrains heritage practices'.[16]

This authorised heritage discourse is one of the factors in the failure of existing legal systems to provide effective recognition and protection for Indigenous peoples' rights and interests in heritage and environment. The fundamental problem is the denial, diminishment or erasure of Aboriginal First Law and Indigenous values in the entire process of management, governance and regulation of places, sites and areas.

Inadequate Provisions for Indigenous Decision-Making and Consent Processes

One of the further factors is the systemic demotion of Aboriginal First Law rights and values vis-à-vis Australian Western law rights and priorities under heritage, mining and planning laws.

---

[15] De Sousa Santos (2016), p. 18.

[16] Waterton and Smith (2010), p. 12.

The recent destruction of 46,000-year-old caves of deep significance to local Aboriginal people at Juukan Gorge in the Pilbara region of Western Australia Aboriginal site exemplifies the failure of existing laws, policies and practices in recognising and safeguarding Indigenous law, culture and heritage. Many of the submissions to the Australian Parliament's Joint Standing Committee on Northern Australia Inquiry into the matter drew attention to the failures and inadequacies of the processes under State and Federal heritage and environment laws. One key aspect concerns the inadequacies, and/or absence of, provisions for equitable Indigenous decision-making, and free, prior and informed consent, compounded by the primacy given to decision-making at Ministerial and bureaucratic levels. A submission from the Gomerai Traditional Custodians, for example (Submission No. 148), highlights the trauma and distress for these people resulting from the decision made by the Federal Environment Minister not to protect important Gomerai cultural sites threatened by mining:

> In Australia, the colonial and post-colonial architectures, places and histories are protected. Both through legislation codes and trusts. However, in Australia in our experience, when it comes to the protection of Aboriginal culture and heritage and sacred places, these protections are not afforded to our people or to our places. Instead, the state protections are turned off with the stroke of a pen by declaring a state project under Planning and the NSW Planning and Assessment commission is put into place to sit and listen to views. Once this occurs the right to appeal through legal process is switched off with no legal course to challenge the decisions or the standard or quality of the archeological books (which in many instances are glaringly failing to demonstrate the policies and Burra charter standards we are told are in place to protect our culture and heritage). After this traumatic process, we as a people have only one recourse to seek protection under the Commonwealth Aboriginal Torres Strait Islander Heritage Protection Act.[17]

The Gomerai Submission continues:

> We, the Gomeroi Traditional Custodians (over 600 signature ATSHIP Application people, supported by the Gomeroi Native Title Applicants on behalf of some 15,000 peoples) and multi-nations (Aboriginal peoples) who have a cultural impact directly to them if the songline is destroyed, blindly and naively put our trust in the ATSHIP system, believing that the Act and its intention as a last resort protection will be able to protect our sacred places, our mortuary trail, multiple burial sites and multiple grinding grooves, a place of post-colonial massacre, a place where the 3rd regiment was deployed to kill our people. Sadly, the ATSHIP Act or more so the Minister representing the Government has been given the power by the elected representatives of modern-day Australia to choose not to protect.[18]

While the flaws in current heritage protection laws may be, at least partly, addressed by developing an entirely new, *sui generis* regime, it is also useful to consider ways in which the current frameworks might be enhanced to provide stronger protection for Indigenous sites, areas and places and to prevent destruction or desecration of these.

---

[17] Parliament of Australia (2020). Submission (No. 148) from the Gomeroi Traditional Custodians to the Australian Parliamentary Joint Standing Committee on Northern Australia Inquiry into the Destruction of 46,000-year-old Caves at Juukan Gorge in the Pilbara Region of Western Australia. Available at: https://www.aph.gov.au/Parliamentary_Business/Committees/Joint/Northern_Australia/CavesatJuukanGorge/Submissions?main_0_content_1_RadGrid1ChangePage=8_20.

[18] Ibid.

Here again, a key aspect to consider is the role of Indigenous participation in, and control over decision-making, and enabling of Indigenous free, prior and informed consent processes.

There are many approaches to heritage, environment and resources management and governance that are discussed in a frame of co-management. Co-management can be one way to incorporate Indigenous perspectives including elements of Indigenous legal systems and decision-making. Yet co-management arrangements have also been subject to critique in regard to the privileging of dominant 'authorised' heritage regulation and management regimes. Grey and Kuokkanen (2020), for example, examine the co-management of Indigenous peoples' cultural heritage in terms of its role in what they regard as 'simultaneously a driver and a product of the culturalization of Indigenous peoples'.[19]

Here, 'culturalization' refers to 'a common practice and strategy of emphasising cultural identity and cultural difference over legal and political status, which essentialises Indigenous peoples and reduces Indigenous rights to minority rights'.[20] These authors explain their critique in the following way:

> Arising from the intersecting discourses/practices of "culture", "heritage", and "management" (…) co-management has been characterised as a defensibly imperfect, "tweakable" system that provides important dividends to both Indigenous and state parties, while additionally building a more productive and respectful relationship between the two.[21]

But to counter these views, Grey and Kuokkanen argue that co-management approaches sit within a dominant neo-liberal and settler-colonial framework, aligned with 'authorised' cultural heritage discourses, and are therefore fundamentally incompatible with Indigenous worldviews. The 'authorised' cultural heritage discourse, they assert, 'cannot escape its founding in powerful concepts that are ontologically, epistemologically and axiologically incompatible with—and in fact hostile to—Indigenous peoples' social and political thought'.[22]

These authors state that 'the protection mechanisms that arise from this discourse are not only theoretically and practically ineffective in Indigenous contexts, they are opposed to the effective preservation and promotion of Indigenous peoples' cultural heritage' and that 'cultural heritage can only thrive by being actively engaged with in situ: on Indigenous lands, through Indigenous institutions'.[23] In their critique, co-management, as an 'authorised' cultural heritage discourse, is 'part of a globally-diffused approach, enshrined in the World Heritage Convention, that offers mere participation in lieu of actual control, while culturalizing and instrumentalising Indigenous polities and rights'.[24]

Recognising the inadequacies in existing legal systems, what are some of the possibilities and options that can be pursued to enable more effective protection and

[19] Grey and Kuokkanen (2020), p. 919.

[20] Ibid.

[21] Ibid.

[22] Ibid., pp. 919–920.

[23] Ibid., p. 920.

[24] Ibid.

recognition of Indigenous values, Laws, rights and interests in heritage and environment? We discuss elsewhere in this book, some important avenues to pursue, such as Earth Laws, and biocultural rights. In this section we review some other examples from the literature that illustrate ways that Indigenous peoples are drawing on their Laws, practices and values, either through working with existing legal systems, or in more innovative ways that foreground Indigenous Law.

A submission from the Central Land Council (Submission No. 109.1) to the Juukan Gorge Inquiry provides one example where existing legal frameworks can offer more effective protection of heritage and culture. This is in the Northern Territory, where Aboriginal sites are generally afforded more protection than in other jurisdictions, under the consent provisions of the *Aboriginal Land Rights Act*. The CLC submission explains this:

> Under section 23(1)(ba) of the *Aboriginal Land Rights (Northern Territory) Act 1976* (Cth) (ALRA), the CLC has a statutory function to assist Aboriginal people in taking measures to protect sacred sites. In performance of this function, the CLC is able to negotiate agreements with proponents that implement robust sacred site protection measures, whether or not on Aboriginal land. CLC records indicate that site damage on Aboriginal land (and other land on which the CLC has exercised its function to assist in protection of sacred sites) occurs only occasionally, with approximately one instance of site damage every 5 years and 2-3 investigations into alleged site damage annually.
>
> It is our view that this reasonably low figure is the result of the CLC's functions under ALRA that enable it to make land access agreements and assist in the protection of sites. These agreements place a positive obligation on agreement holders to obtain sacred site clearances before undertaking activity. The sacred site clearance processes (described in paragraphs [31]–[33] of our submission), allow traditional owners to provide their free, prior and informed consent for any development proposals, providing certainty for all parties.[25]

A submission (Submission No. 108.0A) from the Martuwarra Fitzroy River Council to the Juukan Gorge Inquiry offers a useful frame for seeing how protection and management of a major Aboriginal heritage place (the Fitzroy River—known as the RiverOfLife, Martuwarra—and its catchment areas) is achieved from an Aboriginal perspective.[26] This Martuwarra Fitzroy River Council submission offers their Conservation and Management Plan for the National Heritage Listed Fitzroy River Catchment Estate (July 2020) to show the work of Aboriginal governance for this vitally important riverine ecosystem. The Plan states that 'for Traditional Owners, the health of the River and its connections to Land, nature and livelihoods is central to

---

[25] Parliament of Australia (2020). Submission (No. 109.1) from the Central Land Council to the Australian Parliamentary Joint Standing Committee on Northern Australia Inquiry into the Destruction of 46,000-year-old Caves at Juukan Gorge in the Pilbara Region of Western Australia. Available at: https://www.aph.gov.au/Parliamentary_Business/Committees/Joint/Northern_Australia/CavesatJuukanGorge/Submissions?main_0_content_1_RadGrid1ChangePage=8_20.

[26] Parliament of Australia (2020). Submission (No. 108.OA) from the Martuwarra Fitzroy River Council to the Australian Parliamentary Joint Standing Committee on Northern Australia Inquiry into the Destruction of 46,000-year-old Caves at Juukan Gorge in the Pilbara Region of Western Australia. Available at: https://www.aph.gov.au/Parliamentary_Business/Committees/Joint/Northern_Australia/CavesatJuukanGorge/Submissions?main_0_content_1_RadGrid1ChangePage=8_20.

their culture, heritage and identity'. The Plan adds that 'Under First Law, Traditional Owners maintain and share sophisticated cultural knowledge and practices, and are empowered as guardians to be the voice of the Living Waters of the Martuwarra and its inalienable right to live and flow'.[27] Governance of this river as a living entity under Aboriginal First Law is the crucial point here and is a good example of developing alternatives to the existing system, which hopefully present opportunities to enable better protection and recognition of Aboriginal heritage.

Another example of Indigenous governance of heritage and environment is from Canada, where First Nations communities are using free, prior and informed consent (FPIC) mechanisms and Indigenous Laws to pursue legal pluralism approaches to water governance. Curran explains that:

> The language of free, prior and informed consent has provided Indigenous communities in Canada with a common international standard through which they can address failures in water governance such as inadequate attention to ecological conditions like environmental flows and exclusion of Indigenous rights to water. First Nations are adopting free, prior and informed consent as a framework through which to evaluate proposals using their own legal and governance processes. Not only do these Indigenous legal processes repoliticize decisions about water on Indigenous terms, but also transform water governance by integrating Indigenous methodologies.[28]

There is a wide range of approaches and methodologies regarding heritage recognition and protection and the intersections with legal systems being proposed by Indigenous scholars and practitioners. Canadian Anishnabe legal expert John Borrows, for example, has examined in detail the complex layers of different legal systems in Canada, including Indigenous Laws. He discusses ways of engaging with an Indigenous jurisprudence based in First Laws that draw from the natural world, alongside other legal systems.[29] He argues that 'certain aspects' of Indigenous legal traditions 'continue to guide Indigenous communities in contemporary settings'.[30] He notes that 'these laws have often been ignored or overruled by non-Indigenous laws … [and] … [T]heir influence has thus been eroded within Indigenous communities'.

Notwithstanding this, he explains, 'they embody precepts and practices that connect Aboriginal and non-Aboriginal Canadians to land in a way that is not always possible under the current administration of the common or civil law'.[31] Borrows discusses what he regards as the present system of 'bi-juridicalism' operating in Canada and advocates for greater recognition and adoption of Indigenous laws in that Country, providing details as to how a legal pluralism can be achieved that incorporates Indigenous legal traditions. He suggests that 'affirmation of Indigenous legal traditions would strengthen democracy in the Country by placing decision-making

[27] RiverOfLife et al. (2020).

[28] Curran (2019).

[29] Borrows (2005). See also Anker (2017).

[30] Ibid., p. 96.

[31] Ibid.

authority much closer to the people within these communities'.[32] He explains this further:

> The recognition of Indigenous legal traditions in the Canadian state is bound to be contested and create difficulties in law and policy. Laws dealing with Indigenous peoples must take account of the totality of cultural practices and expressions that belong to them. Recognising and affirming Indigenous legal traditions would facilitate the rule of law within Indigenous communities as they lived closer to their values and principles. It would enable the exercise of greater responsibility for their affairs and allow them to hold their governments and one another accountable for decisions made within their communities. If properly implemented and harmonized with Canada's other legal traditions, such an approach would be consistent with their human rights as peoples while ensuring that other's rights were not abrogated.[33]

Another way forward to addressing some of the failures of the prevailing systems of heritage and environment management and protection is to re-envisage heritage and environment in more inclusive, holistic framings. We explore these ideas elsewhere in this book in the contexts of understandings of Earth Laws, and Indigenous Laws, and of the intersections between these. A holistic perspective on heritage and environment is also critical in the context of the Anthropocene, the urgency of the human-induced climate crisis calling for a re-attachment of the broken connections between humans and non-humans, between the natural and the human worlds. There is a large body of literature in this area. For example, Harrison is one of many writers offering a critique of the separation between nature and culture, exploring its philosophical and epistemological implications for heritage. In what he sees as an 'ontological politics of heritage', he argues that this 'dissolution' of cultural and natural heritage presents an opportunity to re-conceptualise heritage.[34]

Harrison defines heritage as 'a series of diplomatic properties that emerge in the dialogue of heterogeneous human and non-human actors who are engaged in practices of caring for and attending to the past in the present'.[35] He seeks to emphasise the plurality and heterogeneity in heritage and posits what he refers to as 'alternative modes of heritage-making'. His aim is to 'provide windows through which to reconsider the assumptions of the universality and homogeneity of existing, dominant (so called 'modern' or 'Western') models of heritage'.[36]

In Harrison's scheme, the critical point is to establish 'dialogical relationships with heritage' as a way to develop potential 'bridges that might be built among heritage and other adjacent fields or domains of practice which touch directly on questions of the relationship between heritage, ecology, sustainability, health, and resilience'.[37] Another critique of current approaches to heritage protection is offered by Davis, who takes up the problem of a predominantly 'museological' approach common

[32] Ibid., p. 221.

[33] Ibid.

[34] Harrison (2015), p. 24.

[35] Ibid.

[36] Ibid., p. 27.

[37] Ibid., p. 28.

in many heritage instruments, and argues for greater emphasis of dialogue.[38] This perspective that advocates engagement with heritage in a plural, multi-dimensional frame, can offer useful insights in re-conceptualising legal protection of heritage and environment.

Analysing current Western law's approach to environment and culture raises a number of key issues and questions. One that stands out, is that the dominant Western legal system appears to lack a capacity or scope for an understanding of, and engagement with, concepts of 'the sacred' and of the intangible, elements that are crucial in Indigenous peoples' worldviews and cosmologies. We ask therefore, what are some of the ways that the prevailing legal system might be re-configured, to give far greater scope for 'seeing' (refer to our earlier remarks about the differences between looking and seeing), valuing and incorporating concepts of Indigenous sacred and other forms of intangible heritage?

Another concern that the literature review draws attention to, as mentioned elsewhere in this book, is the privileging or hegemony of 'authoritative' discourses in heritage and environment, legislative management and protection. Within a dominant neo-liberal framework, the machinery and processes of 'heritage' and 'heritage protection and management' is performed in a Eurocentric (and often patriarchal) context, wherein vested interests predominate, and decision-making is typically carried out through top-down approaches by ministers, and by the state sanctioned machinery of government and bureaucracy, often supported (and funded) by large global and corporate interests. Therefore, critical questions arise, such as for whom is 'protection' being sought, and to what ultimate ends and in whose interests, are avoided or silenced.

Current heritage and environment legislative regimes generally offer little if any scope for plural thinking (including alternative schemes such as polycentric governance, Indigenous, decolonising and anticolonial approaches), for alternative scenarios, for inclusion of free, prior informed consent processes, self-determination in decision-making and recognition of the rights and interests of non-western others. These latter in fact are often 'Othered' by the state sanctioned authorised heritage and environment laws and discourses; that is, they are at best rendered invisible or subordinate, and at worst, managed within an exoticised and/or racialised paradigm.

2.4 The History of Australia's Colonial Legal System

If, as outlined above, the Australian legal system is 'sick' and needs remediating, why is this not recognised within the dominant discourse? It has been said that 'the last thing a fish will notice is water'. In a colonial system, people from the dominant culture are born into a system of law, economics, politics and culture that rarely questions itself, and so for those in the dominant culture it can be difficult at first to

[38] Davis (2008).

see outside that culture. The pathway forward needs Indigenous and non-Indigenous people to work together to explore what decolonising our legal system can look like.

Professor of Race Relations, Yin Paradies, writes that:

> In settler-colonial societies, interest in colonisation is often focused on relatively distant colonial pasts where Indigenous peoples were 'displaced' (and other euphemisms for slavery, rape, torture, murder and genocide), with relatively scant attention paid to ongoing colonial presence/presents in which systemic, structural, physical, epistemic and ontological violence continue to oppress, assimilate and eradicate Indigenous peoples. This has resulted in vast over-representation of Indigenous peoples among, for example, the impoverished, unhealthy, imprisoned and homeless, as well as even greater under-representation among politicians, administrators, the wealthy, influential and famous. For Indigenous peoples from around the world, the 'slow violence' of colonisation exists alongside violent assaults and fatal neglect. There is also a growing realisation of the impossibility of justice through the law, of reconciliation, or of any answers at all from within settler-colonial states.[39]

Reflecting on the points made above by Paradies, on the legacies and traumas of the colonising project, and on the notions of being 'inside', and 'outside' cultural systems, we may consider also different ways of perceiving, understanding, experiencing and being in the world. Different, or indeed, contrasting systems of philosophy and epistemology may bring different ways of seeing, and looking. There is a critical difference between looking and seeing, as noted by Johannes Wolfgang von Goethe (1749–1832), the German poet, literary critic and scientist. In Goethe's phenomenological approach to the study of nature, it was not sufficient to just look at something. Rather, as David Seamon writes, Goethe's method sought to "... understand a thing's meaning through prolonged emphatic looking and seeing grounded in direct experience". Seamon writes that Goethe 'sought to use firsthand encounter directly in a kindly but rigorous way to know the thing *in itself*'.[40] These remarks may be pertinent to a discussion about colonial constraints in legal reforms and the idea of a kind of 'colonial blindness'. We briefly return to this point in our review of legal pluralism below, with reference to the blinkered view of colonial states in recognising Indigenous rights and legal systems.

The colonial experience then, and its concomitant dominant legal system, has continued to be a fundamental underpinning of the lived experiences and thinking of Indigenous leaders, writers and activists, including those who are among the authors of this book. The concerns flowing from the traumas of colonialism and dispossession provide an excellent foundation upon which to build an evidence base for advocating and enacting decolonising practices and methodologies. This includes the act of acknowledging the RiverOfLife[41] as principal author and cultural integrity through which all expression is made possible.

In the following part of this section, we provide a brief overview of selected laws and policies created within Australia's colonial system, to control and destroy First Nations' Peoples culture, livelihoods and connection to Country. It includes

---

[39] Paradies (2020), p. 438.

[40] Seamon (1998), 536, p. 2, italics in original.

[41] Also known as Martuwarra RiverOfLife.

references to laws that allowed the removal of First Peoples from their lands and from each other and laws that allowed the practices of slavery and Blackbirding in Australia, which continue to affect Pacific communities to this day. This information is just a 'skeletal summary' of some of the complexities of colonisation of Australia. There is a great deal of work that must be done, by non-Indigenous people working in partnership with Indigenous advisors and decolonising experts, to understand the mechanics of decolonisation.[42]

An Overview of Selected British and Australian Laws Created to Control Indigenous Peoples in Australia Since 1788—With a Focus on Commonwealth and Queensland Laws as Examples

With the colonisation of Australia after 1788, a new legal regime was applied, based on the common law. The British Colonial Office treated Australia, for the purposes of its acquisition and the application of English law, as a settled colony, that is, one *uninhabited by a recognised sovereign or by a people with recognisable institutions and laws*. Thus, there were no treaties concluded with any Aboriginal peoples, and no arrangements were made with them to acquire their Land or to regulate dealings between them and the colonists.[43]

Macquarie's famous *Proclamation to the Aborigines of 4 May 1816* is ambivalent as to whether Aborigines were to be considered British subjects, subject to British law. The proclamation imposed certain restrictions upon Aborigines and stated that those who wished to be considered under the protection of the British government and who were 'disposed to conduct themselves in a peaceful, inoffensive, and honest manner' would, upon application to the Secretary's office, be provided with a passport signed by the Governor which would entitle them to protection so long as they did not break his regulations against carrying arms. This in effect made protection of the law for an Aboriginal person a privilege to be granted or withheld at the Governor's discretion. Macquarie's Proclamation of 1816 also represented the first explicit regulation of Aboriginal traditional practices as such. The Proclamation prohibited Aborigines from carrying any spears and prohibited them from pursuing their customary punishment against transgressors of customary law at or near Sydney or other settlements, stating that such practices were repugnant to British laws.[44]

In 1837, the British House of Commons examined the conditions of Aboriginal peoples in British settlements. The Committee in its Report in 1837 recognised the

---

[42] There is a vast and growing literature on Australian colonial history and Indigenous peoples. Among some of the seminal works are those of historians Henry Reynolds, and Bain Attwood, to name just two prominent writers. See for example Henry Reynolds, *Aboriginal Sovereignty: Three Nations, One Australia?*, St. Leonards, NSW, Allen & Unwin, 1996; Bain Attwood, *Empire and the Making of Native Title: Sovereignty, Property and Indigenous People*, Cambridge, Cambridge University Press, 2020.

[43] Australian Law Reform Commission (August 2010). Recognition of Aboriginal Customary Laws—Book 31. Available at: https://www.alrc.gov.au/publication/recognition-of-aboriginal-customary-laws-alrc-book-31/4-aboriginal-customary-laws-and-anglo-australian-law-after-1788/australian-law-as-applied-to-aborigines/.

[44] Ibid.

absurdity and injustice inherent in applying British notions of law automatically to Aboriginal people. However, the Committee reaffirmed the position that Aborigines should be subject to that law.[45]

In 1897 the Queensland Parliament passed The *Aboriginals Protection and Restriction of the Sale of Opium Act*. It was the first instrument of separate legal control over Aboriginal peoples and was more restrictive than any contemporary legislation operating in other states. It allowed the 'Chief Protector' to remove Aboriginal people from their traditional homes and lands, onto and between reserves, and to control the movement of all Aboriginal people deemed to be 'under the Act'. It allowed government bureaucrats to remove children from their families, and despite a range of amendments throughout the first half of the twentieth century, until 1965, the Director of Native Welfare was the legal guardian of all 'Aboriginal' children whether their parents are living or not.[46]

On 23 December 1901 the *Immigration Restriction Act* came into law. It had been among the first pieces of legislation introduced to the newly formed federal parliament. The legislation was specifically designed to limit non-British migration to Australia. It represented the formal establishment of the White Australia policy. This idea focused particularly on people of Asian descent but applied to all non-whites, including Indigenous Australians, who were considered a 'dying race'.[47]

The *Commonwealth Franchise Act* of 1902 gave women the right to vote, but excluded voting by 'Aboriginal natives of Australia'. However, provisions allowed Indigenous persons to vote if they were allowed to vote at state elections prior to Federation under section 41 of the Constitution. The Indigenous franchise was further reduced in practice by admitting only those Aboriginal people already enrolled in a State in 1902. This legislation resulted from the then accepted 'White Australia' policy that was implemented across the nation. Prior to Federation, only New South Wales, Victoria, South Australia and Tasmania extended the franchise to Aboriginal people.

In 1904, regulations made under the 1897 *Queensland Act* (referred to above) were put in place providing for the wages of Aboriginal people to be paid directly to protectors. This legislation, combined with a range of government regulations, created the stolen wages cases that Indigenous people brought later in the twentieth century.[48]

In 1934, the *Aboriginals Protection and Restriction of the Sale of Opium Acts Amendment Act* (Qld) of 1934 extended voting disqualifications via Sect. 2.4 which introduced a new artificial racial category called 'cross breed'. The term was used to describe some Pacific Islanders, as well as those who lived or associated with

[45] Ibid.

[46] Australian government, 'Bringing them Home', see https://bth.humanrights.gov.au/significance/historical-context-the-stolen-generations.

[47] National Museum of Australia (2021). Available at: https://www.nma.gov.au/defining-moments/resources/white-australia-policy.

[48] Parliament of Australia, op. cit.

Aborigines. Under this legislation, anyone the Chief Protector of Aborigines deemed in need of control or 'protection' was also excluded from voting.

By the 1960s, although no formal Indigenous suffrage movement evolved in Australia, several organisations formed to champion the rights of Indigenous people, including voting rights. Such groups included the Federal Council for Aboriginal Advancement (later FCAATSI) and the Queensland Cairns Aboriginal and Torres Strait Islanders (QCAATI). At QCAATI's first conference held in Cairns in July 1960, a Declaration of Rights of the Queensland Aborigines and Torres Strait Islanders was established. The rights included Land rights, unrestricted right of movement, self-government of the islands, missions and settlements, compensation and royalties for mineral extraction and the right of individuals to own and control Land.[49]

In 1965, the *Aborigines' and Torres Strait Islanders' Affairs Act* (Qld) was passed, providing for the management of reserves and welfare for Indigenous persons. It repealed the 1939 legislation. The government of the day said that under the 1965 legislation, the abandonment of protection as a policy was achieved and a new phase of assimilation began. Several legal restrictions on Indigenous peoples remained. This legislation also led to the creation of the Queensland Department of Aboriginal and Islander Affairs.

From the late 1950s, government decisions regarding immigration and other matters began to erode the White Australia policy, until its basic dismantling by the Holt government in 1966. The Whitlam government eliminated it in the 1970s with the introduction of policies like the *Racial Discrimination Act 1975*.[50]

On 27 May 1967, Australians voted to change the Constitution so that like all other Australians, Aboriginal and Torres Strait Islander peoples would be counted as part of the population and the Commonwealth would be able to make laws for them. A resounding 90.77 per cent said 'Yes' and every single state and territory had a majority result for the 'Yes' vote. It was one of the most successful national campaigns in Australia's history.[51]

In 1992, Mabo v Queensland (No. 2) (commonly known as *Mabo*) was a landmark case brought by Eddie Mabo against the State of Queensland. In its decision, the High Court of Australia held that property ownership in accordance with Indigenous customary laws was to be recognised by Australian courts at common law. Prior to *Mabo*, it was commonly assumed that the pre-colonial property interests of Indigenous Australians were not recognised by the Australian legal system. This assumption derived from the legal doctrine of *terra nullius* which was relied upon as a racist legal fiction to import the laws of England across the continent of Australia; in spite of its existing inhabitants.[52]

---

[49] Queensland Parliament, Everyone's Parliament. Factsheet 10.5: *Indigenous Suffrage Timeline—Queensland.* https://www.parliament.qld.gov.au/documents/explore/education/factsheets/Factsheet_10.5_IndigenousSuffrageTimeline.pdf.

[50] National Museum of Australia, op. cit.

[51] AIATSIS. *The 1967 Referendum.* Available at: https://aiatsis.gov.au/explore/1967-referendum.

[52] *Mabo v Queensland (No. 2)* [1992] HCA 23, (1992) 175 CLR (3 June 1992), High Court.

The United Nations Committee on the Elimination of Racial Discrimination ('CERD') determined on 18 March 1999 that the *Native Title Amendment Act 1998* (Cth) *('Native Title Amendment Act')* [known as the 10 Point Plan introduced by Prime Minister John Howard] discriminates against Indigenous title holders by validating past acts, extinguishing native title, upgrading primary production and restricting the right to negotiate ('RTN').

2.5 New Objectives for Australia's Legal System

2.5.1 Duly Recognise, Protect and Enforce First Law in the Australian Legal System

First Law needs to be duly implemented by fully recognising pre-existing First Law rights and interests.

As noted elsewhere in this book, First Law is the 'Law of the Land', not the 'law of humankind'. First Law is about the collective, not the individual. It is about common treasures and responsible use of shared resources. It is founded on laws of relationships and principles of ethics such as respect, reciprocity, care and interdependency with nature.

Its implementation involves a system of kinship with non-human beings, and the inheritance of communal proprietary and individual usufructuary rights and obligations, entrenched in the form of shared totemic ancestors and life forms, Dreamings[53] (Jukurrpa) and Songlines that serve to teach and convey First Law from generation to generation. This includes First Law's unique ways of seeing the world (ontologies) and ways of knowing (epistemologies).

Managing the common treasures for the First Nation group and the individuals involves guardianship, intergenerational responsibility and precautionary stewardship to maintain the balance and harmony of these natural systems and relationships.[54]

Deborah Bird Rose explains that the analysis of common property regimes brings a vital perspective to how the symmetry of First Law principles work:

> (...) that usufructuary rights are embedded within regimes of responsibility, and that regimes of rights and regimes of management are inseparable. Without rights, resources will not be managed; without management, resources will be degraded and depleted, and rights will become meaningless.[55]

[53] Cliff Goddard et al. (2015), op. cit., citing Nicholls (2014, p.5) who argues: "Unfortunately, the dream-related terminology serves to erase the complexities of the original concepts in the many different Indigenous languages and cultures, by emphasising their putatively magical, fantastic and illusory attributes, when the *Jukurrpa, Altyerr, Ungud, Ngarrankarni, Manguny, Wongar,* and so forth are understood by their diverse Aboriginal adherents to be reality, religion, and the Law".

[54] RiverOfLife et al., op. cit.

[55] Bird Rose, D., op. cit.

As all of these characteristics form the essence of First Law, these fundamental rights, interests, relationships and authorities ***must be duly recognised, protected and enforced*** under the Australian common law, as part of the Australian legal system. This is discussed and evidenced in greater detail below.

Implementing First Law will become increasingly achievable once the Australian Western law is re-balanced and re-aligned with First Law by resurrecting the 'Rule of Law' in our Western law and invoking equity, so that the two systems are not just side by side, but also headed in the same broad direction philosophically.

2.6 Embed Principles Consistent with First Law Within the Australian Policy-Making Framework

Principles consistent with First Law perspectives (Indigenous ethics) need to be embedded within the Australian law and policy-making framework.

In this way, ethics and wisdom will also be internalised within the government policy and law design of Australian Western law. This includes fiscal and budgetary laws and policies that influence the economic system.

According to global research,[56] the world's biggest industrialised economies (the G7 nations) will lose 8.5% of GDP each year (or nearly $5 trillion), within the next 30 years from climate change impacts if temperatures rise by 2.6 °C, which they are likely to on the basis of current government pledges and policies under the Paris Agreement. Australia will be hit significantly harder and will suffer a loss of 12.5% of GDP per year by 2050.

A new policy-making framework is clearly required so that our future economic policy, fiscal laws and budgetary decisions can achieve a sustainable business model. Once the new Australian laws are assessed under an ethical and values-based framework, they will be more 'fit for purpose'. This will re-calibrate the economic compass. It will also be much more likely for legal practitioners, businesses and the judiciary to interpret and apply the laws in the future in a way that gives sustainable outcomes for Indigenous peoples and all citizens, because this will be the manifest and express intention of the laws assessed and enacted under this ethical framework.

Here is a diagrammatic representation of the three goals in action and what the transformation looks like, from the status quo legal system—a sick, dislocated and disoriented Western legal system (Fig. 2.1), to the desired state of a healthy, harmonious and wise plural Australian legal system (Fig. 2.2).

In summary, the Australian Western law has become untethered and has gone off-course, taking our society and environment off the rails with it. This is because

[56] Swiss Re Institute (April 2021). *The economics of climate change: no action not an option.* Available at: https://www.swissre.com/dam/jcr:e73ee7c3-7f83-4c17-a2b8-8ef23a8d3312/swiss-re-institute-expertise-publication-economics-of-climate-change.pdf.

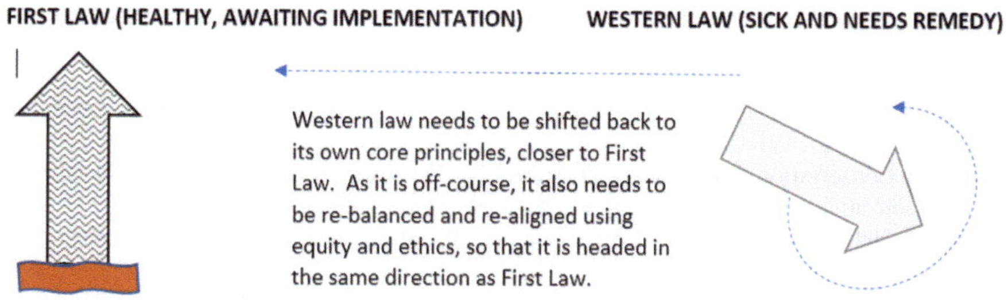

Fig. 2.1 First Law and Western Law, Off Course

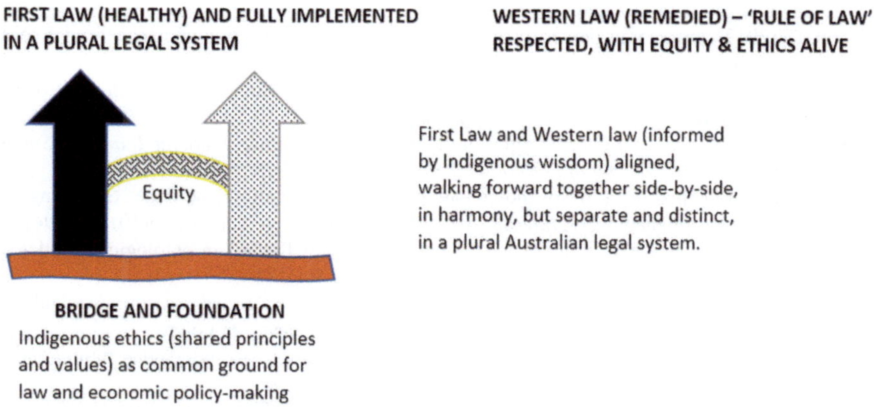

Fig. 2.2 First Law and Western Law, Aligned

the Australian Western law is sick and needs healing. Australia's 'Rule of Law' has been corrupted. Western law has several good components that have gone into a state of disuse, decay and decline, such as equity and other core guiding principles, which are explored further below.

These principles that have been 'missing ingredients', which, once they are added back into use in the Australian Western law, will operate as a remedy and realign it. Its direction will be recalibrated in parallel with First Law, and its relative position vis a vis First Law will be shifted closer to First Law. These principles are essential for environmental and human wellbeing to be served by our legal system—See Fig. 2.1.

Once the Australian Western law is more aligned with First Law principles, it will then be positioned to walk forward with First Law side by side together in harmony in a plural legal system. First Law and Australian Western law will sit on a foundation of shared principles and values (Indigenous ethics) embedded in the legal system. These principles are derived from Country and need to be entrenched into the policy and decision-making powers and duties.

References

Anker, K. (2017). Law as forest: Eco-logic, stories and spirits in indigenous jurisprudence. *Law Text Culture, 21*, 191–213.

Australian Conservation Foundation (ACF). (2021). *ACF wins court case on Adani's water scheme.* Available at: https://www.acf.org.au/acf-wins-court-case-on-adani-water-scheme

Australian National Audit Office (ANAO). (2020). *Award of funding under the community sport infrastructure program.*

Borrows, J. (2005). Indigenous legal traditions in Canada. *Washington University Journal of Law & Policy, 19*, 167–224.

Brennan, G. (2021). Obnoxious cruelty towards Tamil girls is un-Australian. *Sydney Morning Herald*. Available at: https://www.smh.com.au/national/nsw/obnoxious-cruelty-towards-tamil-girls-is-un-australian-20210609-p57ziq.html

Curran, D. (2019). Indigenous processes of consent: Repoliticising water governance through legal pluralism. *Water, 11*(3), 10.

Davis, M. (2008). Indigenous knowledge: Beyond protection, towards dialogue. *The Australian Journal of Indigenous Education, 37*(Supplement), 25–33.

de Sousa Santos, B. (2016). Epistemologies of the South and the future. *From the European South: A Transdisciplinary Journal of Postcolonial Humanities, 1*, 17–29.

Grey, S., & Kuokkanen, R. (2020). Indigenous governance of cultural heritage: Searching for alternatives to co-management. *International Journal of Heritage Studies, 26*(10), 919–941.

Harrison, R. (2015). Beyond "natural" and "cultural" heritage: Toward an ontological politics of heritage in the age of Anthropocene. *Heritage & Society, 8*(1), 24–42.

National Museum of Australia. (2021). *Defining moments: White Australia policy.* Available at: https://www.nma.gov.au/defining-moments/resources/white-australia-policy

Paradies, Y. (2020). Unsettling truths: Modernity, (de-)coloniality and Indigenous futures. *Postcolonial Studies*. https://doi.org/10.1080/13688790.2020.1809069

RiverOfLife, M., Poelina, A., Alexandra, J., & Samnakay, N. (2020). Conservation and Management Plan for the National Heritage Listed Fitzroy River Catchment Estate, p. 5. Available at: https://researchonline.nd.edu.au/nulungu_books/1/

Seamon, D. (1998). Goethe, nature, and phenomenology: An introduction. In D. Seamon & A. Zajonc (Eds.), *Goethe's way of science: A phenomenology of nature* (pp. 1–14). State University of New York Press.

Twomey, A. (2021). Constitutional risk: Disrespect for the rule of law and democratic decay. *The Canadian Journal of Comparative and Contemporary Law, 7*, 293–341.

Waterton, E., & Smith, L. (2010). The recognition and misrecognition of community heritage. *International Journal of Heritage Studies, 16*(1–2), 4–15.

Yunkaporta, T., & Kelleher, M. (2021). *First law and songlines: The other others.* [Podcast]. With Mary Graham & Dr. Anne Poelina. Available at: https://open.spotify.com/episode/3q0WY4VBhhs38iHTtTA3Nd

Chapter 3
Personal Stories

In order to share glimpses into the richness and diversity of Indigenous cultures in Australia, we, as the collective authors of this work, who include Indigenous elders and community leaders (operating as a Think Tank of ideas), share stories of the harm done by colonisation and the enforcement of colonial laws. The Indigenous authors of this work are also sharing their personal reflections of what it means to be 'governed' by the laws of nature that embrace the interconnectedness and complexity of human—nature interactions. These stories serve to reinforce that the ongoing practice of colonial law, which partitions and segregates nature into component parts (land, air, water, soil, ocean) is ill-equipped to adequately represent First Nations interests until there is a system of legal pluralism which recognises First Laws—what is often referred to in the Western legal literature as 'customary laws'.[1]

This book recognises the diversity of Indigenous cultures, languages, societies and experiences, and that it is therefore not possible (or appropriate) to define First Laws, or Earth laws, through a singular or homogenous frame.[2] There are a number of overarching principles of First Law and Earth Laws which are defined below.

The stories presented here highlight the ongoing impacts of the colonial legal system and culture, and what is required to take the necessary steps to ensure we create a legal and moral pathways to understand, critique and respond to the true history of colonisation in Australia. The book includes suggestions about how to achieve this goal.

These stories give substance to our proposal that the Australian Nation State should embrace legal pluralism; be an advocate for deconstructing the harmful elements of colonial law, and be a strong proponent for the recognition of customary laws in

[1] See, for example, Tobin (2014).

[2] The vexed issue of 'defining' Indigenous concepts, including what some refer to as 'customary law', goes to important questions of 'who is doing the defining', and related matters of self-determination, including the right for Indigenous peoples to define their own concepts, categories and philosophical traditions.

A. Poelina et al., *Declaration of Peace for Indigenous Australians and Nature*,
https://doi.org/10.1007/978-981-99-9327-7_3

statute. Only when this occurs will First Nations rights be adequately protected and legitimised through the practice of common law.

3.1 Questions that Guided the Case Studies and Stories

In shaping these stories, which are a mix of personal reflections, collections of vignettes and literature review, the composite of stories was guided by the following questions:

1. What is your lived experience, knowledge and or practice of First Law (customary law or traditional law), and what are the lessons to share with our Nation?
2. How can this wisdom of First Law influence legal pluralism?
3. How can we advocate and create legal and other institutional systems which give effect to peace with nature and with Indigenous peoples?

3.2 Indigenous First Laws—Summary of Principles

> First Nations Peoples' law is of the beginning: of the first songs, sung by the ancestors. When the first steps were walked across the ruwe, Country was sung into creation. Law conceived as a way of living is difficult to write about and cannot simply be described or easily translated into a foreign language that is empty of the ideas that our law ways carry. Our law was not written in the way in which the West conceives of writing. Law was painted in ceremonial design and symbols were marked on boundary markers, identifying traditional owners and their ngaitjis. The differences between Nunga and non-Aboriginal legal systems are so extensive that there is no basis upon which comparison can be drawn ...... (Aboriginal) law is the essential basis of social conduct: respect, reciprocity and caring for Country to name a few. These ethical principles convey the essential nature of the law.[3]

Summarising from the stories in this section, a number of principles and concepts can be gleaned about the underpinning elements of Indigenous First Law. These are presented below as an indicative sample but should not be considered as being comprehensive nor universally agreed upon by Australian First Nations peoples.

From Mary Graham's Story

- The Land (Country) is the source of the Law and it places on humans an obligation to look after the Land for future generations '*Look after Country, look after Kin*'.
- Land is a creator of all life which then sets social and behavioural rules for humans to follow '*I am located therefore I am*'.
- The life force in all its forms and with other human groups is based on Relationality rather than Survivalism.
- Relationality of humans with the Land determines culture, which is a tool to achieve (and maintain) coherence about human relationship to, and understanding

[3] Watson (2015), p. 22.

of, the environment, other humans and collectives. Place defines identity and culture.
- Culture creates security based on Coherence, Proportionality, Predictability = Effective Personal and Communal Security = Relationality.
- This recognises that there is a two-way system (two-way learning) or Autonomous Regard which is respectful, restrained, considered and discreet; it isn't the equivalent of the board game-like strategic autonomy.
- This forces long-term strategic thinking favouring reciprocity, in preference to a 'winner-takes-all' or survivalist approach to governing typical of Western systems.
- Humans are ultimately, inextricably and will forever be obliged to Land for our existence—a Custodial Ethic.

From Dr. Anne Poelina's Story

- Aboriginal identity is shaped by a world view (an ethos) of 'we and not me'.
- Rivers (the Martuwarra, the River of Life, as a place) form identity, spirituality and Law (Warloongarriy Law).
- Ancient stories are teachings of values, ethics, code of conduct and how to live in a civil society. They encompass teachings based on science, but which is not recognised in a colonial construct of scientific knowledge. In the case of Rivers, surface water and ground water are part of the same system created by the Rainbow Serpent sustaining human and non-human beings.
- First Law should be the foundation for developing State law (not the other way around)—social, economic and environmental elements are all intertwined—not discrete elements to be 'balanced' or traded off.
- Indigenous people hold knowledge which is important to be considered in decision-making (including in law reform). Decision-making should be informed through regional governance approaches. Collective wisdom of Indigenous science and First Law can empower ways of postmodern living by re-examining human-earth relations.
- Sustainable life is not the same as sustainable development—the latter being to promote economic growth with little regard for inherent limitations of ecological systems.
- It is time to stop 'othering' Indigenous people as their knowledge is a gift of ancient wisdom.

From Ross Williams' Story

- Accentuates the concept of Relationality and identity defined by place to encompass not just Land as a terrestrial notion as viewed in Western constructs, but to also include ocean, water, flora, fauna, sky and each other.
- Earth Law knowledge is retained in many ways including by story holders, the holders of law, cultural storytellers, the holder and practitioners of songlines, sacred and secret knowledge holders, clan knowledge holders and language keepers and speakers, the teachers both men and women, teachers for and of Country in its holistic form, being the essence of learning.

- The Land has memory which can permit healing. Permission to burn (for healing) comes from the Land not from 'Land management authorities'.
- Nature provides signs which tell us when and where it is the right time to interact and or partake. First Law is universal through time (fixed)—it does not change like colonial law.

From Dr. Chels Marshall's Story

- Language, culture and Land are connected, and this conveys the knowledge of sustainable healthy functioning ecosystems (Dreamtime stories and Songlines carry meaning and knowledge).
- Indigenous perspectives provide balance to colonial historic and contemporary research, writings and design.

From Tyson Yunkaporta's Story

- Law (Bora Bora) is the same everywhere.
- Nothing is created or destroyed—just transformed. Thus, everything is self-sustaining and interconnected making natural systems sentient beings.

From Donna Bagnall's Story

- The world is made up of complex, dynamic systems within systems of which people are a part of.
- Songlines, Jukurrpa (Dreaming) and totems are a common property institution for long-term ecological management and convey the laws (and can be seen as Statutes).
- Implicit among them are obligations of guardianship, intergenerational responsibility and precautionary stewardship to maintain the balance and harmony of natural systems and relationships.
- The past is to be used in the present moment to protect the future.
- First Laws are, in essence, the Constitution and By-laws from the lands and waters. Given that the Laws and People are connected to Land, First Law can never be extinguished.
- Customary law is not an historic artefact as it guides Aboriginal people in fundamental ways in the community on Country and conveys their obligations to look after one another and care for Country.

From Shola Diop's Story

- As a largely dispossessed people with an amalgamation of cultural and linguistic roots, Australian South Sea Islanders struggle with the assertion of any single form of First law.
- An effective through-line for Australian South Sea Islanders emerges in the customary concepts that run consistently across the various Melanesian cultures that we originate from.
- Kastom is a Pijin term that can refer to shared traditions, but also to ideas and institutions perceived to be grounded in Indigenous concepts and principles.

- The term 'kastom' (denoting customary practice) has been used at various times in relation to Australian South Sea Islander relations with their families and nations in the Pacific.

These Indigenous perspectives and lived experiences are written by Indigenous leaders who share their understanding of the complexity of racism and its impacts at personal, community and systemic levels. These authors remain the owners of their stories and retain Indigenous cultural intellectual property (ICIP) right over their stories.

This body of evidence illuminates a multilayered complexity within Aboriginal Nations, providing the opportunity to consider the culturally diverse and distinct relationships with Torres Strait Islander and Pacific Island Nations. This rich insight evidences shared experiences of colonialism as being distinctly different to the Pacific Island context.

3.3 Mary Graham

The Relationist Ethos and the Law of Obligation

Biography

My name is Mary Winifred Graham, I was named after my mother Winifred who was born on Auburn Station in Southern Queensland. She was a Wakka Wakka person who grew up on Cherbourg Aboriginal Settlement formerly known as Barambah. She later lived in Gayndah in the Burnett River region.

My father was Jack Hamilton Graham and his people and traditional Country is the Gold Coast but is known among our Mob as Dangan Bullen Chagun—Land of the five rivers—or technically rivers five Land. The language is Yugambeh and our Mob is the Kombu-merri, we are one of several different groups here in the Gold

Coast region which stretches from the Logan River just south of Brisbane down to the Tweed River and back to the ranges inland. The Nerang River is very special to Kombu-merri.

Here on the Gold Coast our Mob are saltwater people so fishing, crabbing and oystering were the mainstay of food and later as small business to maintain a measure of independence. Dreaming stories were many and varied but one of my favourites were about the Wahjung—dolphins. The people here on the Coast had an agreement with Wahjung that they would help with the fishing by herding the fish in closer to shore where people could easily access them and then sort them out and part of the catch would be shared with Wahjung. One day a man, scooping and catching the herded fish decided not to share with Wahjung, but kept the whole lot for himself and his family. When that happened Wahjung decided to leave, so they went away and never came back, i.e. they came back but not to help with the fishing. From then on catching fish was hard work, that was his punishment for breaking Wahjung Law. The Law was/is about the *relational* and the Law of Obligation that man went against Law. This forms the basis of my story.

I have lectured on subjects in Aboriginal history, politics and comparative philosophy at the University of Queensland and at other educational institutions around the Country. I have produced written materials principally on philosophical and political themes and have published in international journals.

I have held different positions on several community organisations in Brisbane, Queensland State and nationally and also engaged in international research projects involving Australia and the UK. I currently do research work with the Institute of Urban Indigenous Health (IUIH), the leading Aboriginal health organisation in Brisbane.

I have been a Casual Lecturer at the University of Queensland (UQ) in the School of Political Science and International Studies (POLSIS), the School of Psychology and the School of Historical and Philosophical Inquiry.

'The concept and practice of Regenerative Songlines is one of the best ways of strengthening and maintaining the Law of Obligation'

Concept

Because the Land brought us into being and continues to keep us alive and protected, we are forever obliged to look after it, but it is more than a duty, it is brought us into the sacred *relational*, the embedding of ethics, morality and empathy in us, that is, acquiring the condition of being worthy of what is proper.

> **Foundational Principle**—To the extent that the Land is the source of the Law, Aboriginal Australia said to the people: "co-operate, don't compete; share, don't hoard; attend the consensus; extend your relationships; look after Land and Honour your Sacred sites". It is a Law, which requires an ahistorical view of time.[4]

The idea and practice of Obligation gives to human society a greater return, for observance and adherence to the tradition, such as—nourishment/health, meaning, a

---

[4] Graham (2009a).

flourishing society, security, protocols and above all, wellbeing assurance for future generations.

Practice

Law of Obligation is attending to and maintaining the custodial stewardship, ethical obligations of looking after Lands, waters and the wellbeing, cultural, physical and spiritual being and values of all Peoples within our boundaries who have lived in this Country for millennia, continue to, and now, live here and practice stewardship obligation to care for all Lands and Peoples.

> Look after Country, look after Kin. (Old saying)

The Law of Obligation

The Law of Obligation concept and practice defined above emerged out of the relationist connection to Land, seeing Land as the original inventor/creator of all life, environmental and human which gave rise to a unique civilisational culture, which has its own logic, philosophy, values and notions of social development. This is a society and culture of great age and its ethics encompasses not only appropriate social conduct, social and political structure of society, all knowledge (sacred and otherwise), spiritual obligations, but also includes systems of logic, time and space.

Following is a list (by no means exhaustive) of collective terms of reference relating to Laws of Obligation:

- The Custodial Ethic: looking after Country, looking after kin—Stewardship and Reciprocity;
- Relationalism—Autonomy, Balance, Place and Ethics (Law/Songlines);
- Primacy of family, especially children, young and old people;
- Formal age and gender recognition, respect and governance structure;
- Non-hierarchical, gendered governance structures with Elders and knowledgeable people as authority;
- Positive group dynamics, conflict management and non-competitiveness;
- Consensus decision-making and attending to the consensus;
- Careful management of ego[5];
- Land has intrinsic moral and spiritual integrity—Land is the central source of the Law/Lore[6];
- Primacy of place, identity/relationalism and autonomy as an organising principle;
- Aboriginal system of logic, multi-dimensional time (different to Western and Asian systems).

Aboriginal society is a civilisational culture, (not civilisational state), i.e. a socially and politically ordered system with a self-regulated sacralised, ecological, stewardship Law of Obligation. A system that stretched across the whole continent for

[5] The ego is viewed as a potentially volatile substance to be treated with something like a combination of caring stewardship, referee-like supervision and watchful guardianship.

[6] Graham (2014).

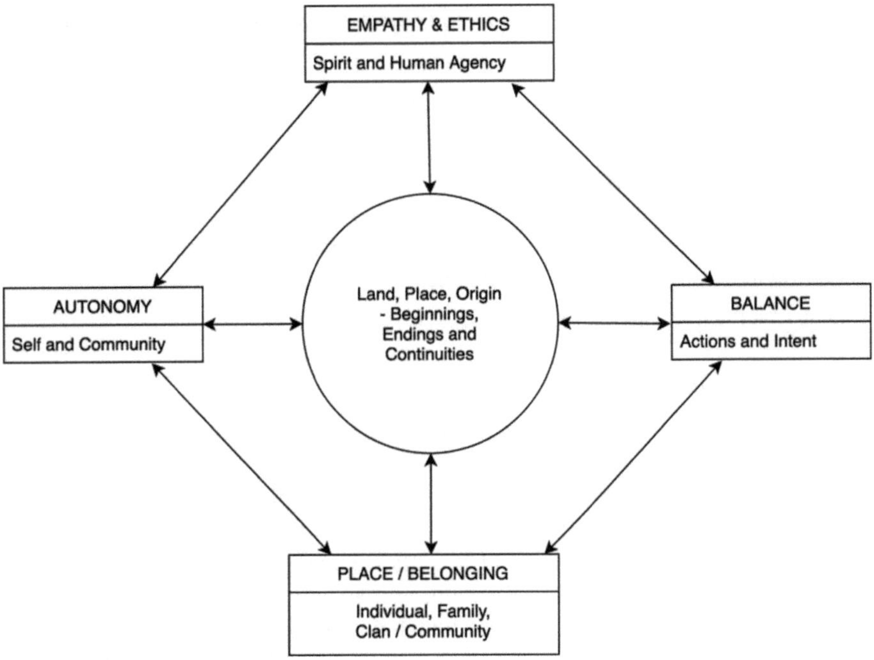

Fig. 3.1 Relationality[7]. Arrows denote critical and variable networks

millenia. The above terms/qualities underpin Aboriginal social praxis and form the ontological and epistemological basis of existence. In this sense, Aboriginal Law/ Aboriginal civilisation could be said to be both an action guide to living and a guide to understanding reality itself, especially in relation to Land as the basis for all meaning. This results in a highly complex but ordered, elegant understanding of existence as shown in Fig. 3.1, far removed from the chaotic and dangerous world of the short-term survivalist ethos.

The critical and variable networks are the vast array of connections—social, cultural, spiritual and psychological that are the conduit for—feeling; positive stability; logic and its suspended judgmentalism; custodial ethos and its moral framework; and congenial fellowship and relationality.

The Land is the source of the Law. Any notion of Aboriginal social and political order has to begin with the Aboriginal relationship to Land. The establishment and maintenance of Relationality rests with its attributes, which are:

---

[7] Ibid.

Autonomy; Place/Identity; Ethics/Custodial Ethic; Balance

Autonomy

Expanding one's sphere of influence by conquest of other Lands does not confer security—just the opposite—it ensures insecurity in a number of ways, not least of which is grievance of long standing of the 'conquered' which may or may not express itself in myriad ways. Coercion in relations sooner or later rebounds—the act(s) of coercion is not forgotten. They are solidly embedded in the narratives of all those involved in conquest projects.

Structure; Non-hierarchical

Place/Identity

Instead of, 'I think therefore, I am'[8] but rather 'I am located therefore I am'—while one has autonomy as a spiritual being inextricably tied to a spiritual landscape, the Aboriginal individuality is not centred on the idea of a rational, autonomous self alone in the world as a discrete entity or conscious isolate searching for meaning.

Balance

Balance is searched for, is necessary and is required for a positive, stable society. Balance is not bending people to one's will but sponsoring and accounting for the interests of others, sharing and being reckoned with. This is what and how one's place in the world is determined not through domination of one's environment. Foreign policy is perpetually a balance between interests and values.

The Law of unintended consequences—very important in Aboriginal Rules of Engagement plus good psychology.

Ethics/Custodial Ethic (Traditionally the Law—An All-Encompassing System)

People have to have some kind of belief system in order to have a spiritual justification for agency. A sense of shame and propriety related to one's conduct.

These terms/qualities underpin the Aboriginal social praxis and ontological and epistemological basis of existence. Humanism is not a unified system, it is a rationalist outlook or system of thought attaching prime importance to human rather than divine or supernatural matters. The rational self is individualistic, self-centred/egotistic.[9]

The system of Relationality or co-existence that was developed among the many groups throughout the whole continent was effective, efficient, rational, stable, sustainable with a meritocratic system of governance and inclusive with an absence of domination by any one group over another or others.

This co-existence was underpinned by the rules of engagement, non-hierarchical social and political structures both within and between clan groups, very different

[8] Descartes (1999).

[9] The ego is seen as a potentially volatile substance to be treated with something like a combination of caring stewardship, referee-like supervision, watchful guardianship and prompts toward attentive, measured persuasion.

notions of power and authority (the two are not conflated in Aboriginal thinking), a preference for territorial integrity rather than the expansion of spheres of control/influence by invading another's Country—the preferred Aboriginal word for one's own Land/territory—or, the impulse to forced clan unification.

Relationality and Survivalism sit beside each other.

Relationality	Relational reasoning	Relational ethos
Lateral organisational structures; Land/environment partnership	Aboriginal logic and the intuitive mind; reflective motive; resource management	Place, autonomy, balance and ethics (the law) Land becomes Country not territory
Survivalism	Survivalist reasoning	Survivalist ethos
Hierarchies; territory/Land and resources capture	Logic; unreflective motive; economic and technological dominance and endless growth	Security guarantee, strategic autonomy and the zero-sum game; Land becomes property/territory

These terms/qualities underpin the Aboriginal social praxis and ontological and epistemological basis of existence.

3.3.1 Relationalism and Survivalism

In looking at an ancient culture and system like Aboriginal society it would be easy to assume a high level of incommensurability between their understanding of principles of organisation and the Western ideas of complex, highly technological systems.

However, like most human groups throughout history, everything starts with some form of guarantee of security for the group and its members. And for Aboriginal people security was to be found in the development of a system of co-existence with the natural environment, i.e. the life force in all its forms and with other human groups based on Relationality rather than Survivalism.

What is the purpose of human culture? It is a tool to achieve (and maintain) coherence about human relationship to, and understanding of, the environment, other humans and collectives. The purpose of culture is to give ourselves purpose, this then gives people the general feeling of confidence that one's environment is predictable. For Aboriginal people this predictability came through the primary relationship between people and Land/environment and secondly the relationship between people or society—the latter was/is always contingent on the first.

If culture is the expression of human attempts to acquire coherence about existence, then, understanding proportionality and predictability, among other factors, are the main pre-requisites for attaining the relational aspect of effective security for both the individual and the collective while living culturally.

The pathway towards achieving personal and social/communal security, that is, the security that is coherent, proportional and predictable is through a measured equilibrium between notions of Relationality and Survivalism.

Coherence, Proportionality, Predictability = Effective Personal and Communal Security = Relationality.

The 'wild card' in this algorithm is the pathway possibilities that any/all crisis/ challenge situations present. Will the long-term or short-term view be taken? Will the strategic or tactical response be more advantageous? Is the relationalist or survivalist ethos preferred, in making these decisions, the more rewarding socially, culturally or otherwise?

- Most people are both Relationalists and Survivalists.
- Some people have the Relationalist Ethos.
- Too many people (and states) have the Survivalist Ethos.

'Aboriginal people, like many Indigenous people around the world, are Relationalist Ethos people'

Survivalism

Ordinary survival (ism) can be both an everyday small event and a large event like a war or pandemic. General survival is—almost getting hit by a bus in traffic, swimming in shark infested waters, and losing one's job after a long career or in an economic downturn. Involvement in large scale events like being a refugee fleeing war/revolution or trying to survive a war-torn impoverished Country. Indigenous people everywhere trying to survive colonialism—in the immediate sense or over centuries.

Survivalism is having an idea of the world and life as a place of constant struggle and/or danger, a permanent striving through life. One could say that people who see themselves as 'battlers' are like 'survivalists', survivalists follow survivalism as a frame of reference even after achieving reasonable or moderate security. Economists and anthropologists have always evinced struggle (the survivalist life) as a natural state of being for the indigent and the Indigenous.

However, the **Survivalist Ethos** arises when individuals, groups or Peoples and states conclude that the hard, relentless experience of fighting for survival in any of the above-named experiences, for any length of time, in any range of different circumstances, *is indeed,* what life is all about. That is, the crucial importance is when the survivalist starts to see the environment, natural and/or social, as inherently hostile and therefore tend to see others (and their actions) as the competitive Other and so becomes alert and wary, i.e. to see only one's self as autonomous and the Other as a potential rival or threat. The whole canon of international relations writing is based on the survivalist ethos, and it can be called strategic autonomy, as in the current European political concept—European Strategic Autonomy (ESA).

Sayings connected to this notion are 'it's a jungle out there', i.e. social and political life itself, 'look after number one', 'get them before they get you', 'it's a dog-eat-dog world' and 'winner takes all'. The more hostility shown and/or experienced, the more anxiety, tension and misgiving rises. The world has turned into an arena.

A survivalist ethos can lead a state to see the global space as a hostile environment and therefore pursue a policy of strategic autonomy, with a moderate but growing nationalist self-regard.

Furthermore, like the survivalist person who runs the risk of becoming an extreme discrete entity or conscious isolate trapped in a hostile world, the state with this ethos imperils itself when their own nationalist self-regard becomes extreme.

Relationalism

Ordinary relationalism or relationality

Because places are related to each other and to people, peoples are also related and hence are not conscious isolates positioned against each other and the world. Instead, they are bound more or less closely or at a distance. Relationalism = families, relations, friends, clans—connected culturally or not, but, connected by Land, Dreaming stories, songlines, narratives and experiences—everyday experiences and large ones like ongoing colonialism and imperialism.

However, the **Aboriginal Relationalist Ethos** arose out of the original relationalist phenomenon of Land creating and growing up humans and humanness, along with humans learning and recognising that humans are autonomous beings. And, by applying concepts such as—the Custodial Ethic to Land and society, the law of obligation (reciprocity etc.) and Autonomous Regard toward others, then long-term stability, a flourishing society and security for future generations are all possible.

Autonomy is valued, but balance is pursued—both among human and other than human forces. The concept and practice of Autonomous Regard (AR) arises out of the Relationalist Ethos. Examples are when Aboriginal people talk of 'two-way learning, two-way governance or two-way health care system, etc.'. Each way of the two-way system is autonomous but willingly engages in walking pathways together, not in a conflated way but in a balanced, distanced way, as peers and equals. The two-way system or Autonomous Regard method is respectful, restrained, considered, discreet etc., it isn't the equivalent of the board game-like strategic autonomy.

Relations among countries/nations are pursued through these same principles. Other nations are naturally other and different because they are of other places. But this does not preclude relations with them because one's Dreaming connects through place(s) with their Dreaming and this facilitates interaction and exchange. This does not eliminate fear and conflict among Aboriginal Australian groups or within groups, but it explains the relative absence of 'survivalist ethos' thinking in the form of security dilemma.

Relationalist Ethos is not 'Kumbayarism'[10] either. It is:

1. *We are not alone in the world*; even if other humans are absent, there are other sentient beings present, ancestral spirits and these have meaning for Aboriginal

[10] Kumbaya is part of an old African-American spiritual song in *Gullah,* a creole language from the Southern Coastal region of Georgia US. Kumbaya translated is '[God or Lord], come by here'.

people. Aboriginal people are not discrete entities living in a hostile environment, neither are they conscious isolates searching for meaning;
2. *The babe in arms requires* more than just its physical needs met, it needs tenderness, affection and speech—it needs the relational; and
3. For Aboriginal people, *standards of behaviour are preceded and shaped by the deep reflective motive,* which is akin to *long-term strategic thinking*, that in turn leads one to a *stewardship frame of mind* which then guides and influences people not only to act positively but to do so willingly. This is preferred to short-term tactical thinking that can lead to instability and disregard for others.

Rejection of the Survivalist Ethos

This is a form of self-orientation where the self is placed at a distance from others because all environments—natural, human and social—are seen as potentially hostile; so, the self has to arm itself psychically and physically to keep 'safe'. Social and technological developments ensue, and then praxis follows which includes the normalisation of competitiveness.

In Aboriginal culture, the survivalist ethos was countered by the deep reflective and relationalist motive, which comes from the sharing of resources, fulfilling one's social obligations, the maintenance of good relations (as much as possible) and diplomatic traditions. This is why the concept of invasion and conquest of other people's country was unknown. The first outcome of this reflection—*the importance of reciprocity*—arose from relating to Land/Nature. This is the great life force that we can touch and feel, but which also looks after all our physical, emotional and spiritual needs.

Conclusion: Relationalism and Survivalism are set in a relational tension in Aboriginal political and social ordering, both underpinned by relational-ecological stewardship. The relationalism mitigates and manages survivalist ethos tendencies and this provides a guide or at least a pathway to properly addressing political and social concerns.

3.3.2 *Coherence—The Beginning of the Reflective Self*

Coherence emerges out of the experience of relating to the Land best expressed in the term—the Land is the Source of the Law.[11] Land invented human beings and other life forms, it is thrown us up into the world and into the imaginative ability to create society and culture, and it helps us (continually) to form society and keeps us alive and creative through its resources, its changes and enabling capacities. We (humans) are ultimately, inextricably and will forever be obliged to Land for our existence.

[11] Black (2011).

The obligation is expressed in broad reciprocal social and cultural arrangements where human collectives—clan and language groups 'look after' Land within particular local regions recognised by other collectives. Arrangements or to be more exact a complex systematisation takes place or to put it another way—the Law, in all its manifestations, enters the world, becomes embedded within and between groups and the world becomes ordered as the following:

- Cultural (narratives, languages, representations, the Custodial Ethic);
- Ceremonial (spiritual integrity, Land as a moral entity, duties to ancestral spirits;
- Practical (attending the consensus, consensus decision-making, primacy of the family, especially children and young people);
- Organisational (Elders are an authority but don't rule: a non-hierarchical structure with men and women in balance);
- Personal (non-competitiveness, maintenance of harmonious relations, careful management of the ego, positive conflict management and group dynamics).

Combined, the above arrangements can also be understood as the Custodial Ethic, such an ethic serves a valuable purpose by suspending social and political judgmentalism, especially between groups, and promotes autonomy.

Proportionality—The Environment of the Reflective Self

How do we measure up in our own Country, i.e. how do we measure ourselves (not in a competitive sense) to/with the Country/landscape/ground itself, to others in and outside the group, to the ancestors, to Spirit Beings? How do we fit in the place and Country we're in, more to the point how do we find this good fit?

The only place to start seems to be the measure utilised by ancestors—how did the ones who went before us do it. If the exact, correct, measured relationship with our surroundings can be understood properly, it can only be in the state of the environment that was left for us to be Custodians. The intention was clear—the Land doesn't actually need any human or particular life form to care for it, and yet here we are—it created us with the most complex and yet the most contradictory qualities and states of being like human will, logic, reflective and unreflective motives, vulnerabilities, fears including a propensity for violence.

Given the state of this contradictoriness of human nature itself, Aboriginal people's development of the Custodial Ethic of looking after Country seems like a path that determined two things—a clarity of purpose as to the meaning and nature of the life force—that it must keep going and that all humans have a vital role to play in this task and—that by undertaking this role we grow and develop ourselves into fully developed human beings, i.e. Lawful Beings.

Within a moral/spiritual landscape the Custodial Ethic has to be maintained by people being lawful, simultaneously the ego, the wild card of human nature, is not deemed to be sinful or bad but seen like a potentially volatile substance to be treated with something like a combination of caring stewardship, referee-like supervision, watchful guardianship and prompts toward attentive, measured persuasion.

The primacy of place, identity and autonomy is shown clearly in the Aboriginal language map—a map that is about more than language but about the representation of a locality based, social and political organising principle rather than an ideological one.

3.3.3 *Predictability—The Reflective Self Challenged*

Aboriginal logic or, if this is too challenging for some, logic with Aboriginal characteristics follows the below organising principles as shown in Fig. 3.2.

Multiple Places = Multiple Dreamings = Multiple Laws = Multiple Truths = Multiple Perspectives = All perspectives (truths) are Valid and Reasonable.[12]

The two systems—*the Custodial Ethic* and *the Logic—all perspectives are valid and reasonable*—are in the Aboriginal context like first principles, i.e. a priori in that they are simply assumed and exist prior to reasoning. The two principles together are very effective—ideally one cannot stand without the other. The logic of 'all perspectives are valid', reasonable on its own, is quite cold blooded and can lead to a kind of extreme relativism where there is no meaning at all especially in regards moral dilemmas or ethical judgements. The logic is an instrument to suspend or soften judgement, aid and sharpen a correct sense of proportionality where good judgement, prudence or discernment are required.

The Custodial Ethic is an ethic of obligation to family, clan, community and Country—the Law of Obligation—involving the vast array of expressions of Aboriginal Lawfulness which is part of the overall solemn and sublime Aboriginal Law covering the whole of existence, time and space.

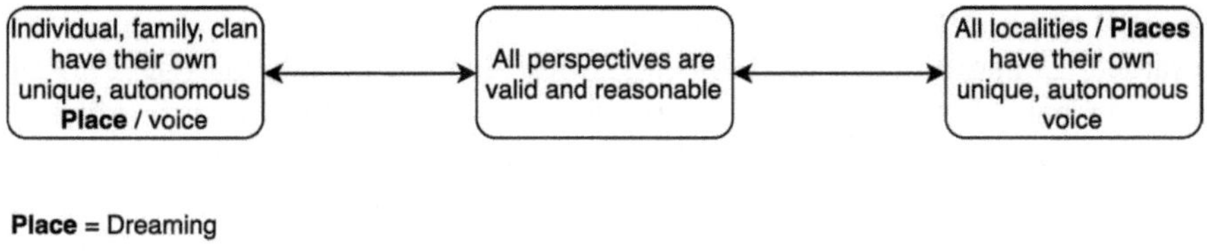

Fig. 3.2 Challenging the reflective self

[12] Graham (2009b).

3.4 Anne Poelina

Narratives of First Law from the Martuwarra Fitzroy River

Biography

Professor Anne Poelina is a Nyikina Warrwa (Indigenous Australian) woman in the Kimberley region of Western Australia. Anne is an active Indigenous community leader, human and Earth rights advocate, filmmaker and a respected academic researcher, with two Doctorates, Master of Public Health and Tropical Medicine, Master of Education and Master of Arts (Indigenous Social Policy). Her second PhD (First Law), awarded in 2021, was titled, '*Martuwarra First Law Multi-Species Justice Declaration of Interdependence: Wellbeing of Land, Living Waters, and Indigenous Australian People*'. Anne was a signatory to the Redstone Statement in 2010 and a 2011 Peter Cullen Fellow for Water Leadership. In 2017, she was awarded a Laureate from the Women's World Summit Foundation (Geneva) and elected Chair of the Martuwarra Fitzroy River Council (2018). She is a Professor, Chair of Indigenous Knowledges and Senior Research Fellow with Nulungu Institute Research, Notre Dame University and a Research Fellow with Northern Australia Institute Charles Darwin University. Anne is also a Visiting Fellow with the Crawford School of Public Policy at the Australian National University which includes being an active member of the Water Justice Hub focusing on Indigenous Water Valuation and Resilient Decision-making.

Professional website: www.martuwarra.org
Personal website www.annepoelina.com
ORCID: https://orcid.org/0000-0001-6461-7681.

3.4.1 *Who Am I?*

Ngayoo yimardoowarra marnin I am a Nyikina Warrwa woman who belongs to the Mardoowarra Fitzroy River, and I live by a Law of Obligation and reciprocity with, and to human and non-human beings. This paper uses the Indigenous methodology of storytelling. I have included poems, films, Songlines and First Law, Law of the Land, Law of Nature to help tell this narrative. It is deliberately not writing in the academic style. The intent for writing this story is to illuminate my insider position, my lived experiences as an Indigenous woman and how my worldview, my values and ethics are framed within a world of 'we' and not 'me'.

In this story I use multiple vignettes to share how Indigenous people are connected through kinship, obligation and our Law of the Land. Together I weave these voices together, all the while acknowledging the authority and authorship of Martuwarra as cited in the footnotes. As the story contains films these films are protected by Indigenous Cultural and Intellectual Property (ICIP) Rights and the filmmaker owns their property. None of the film footage can be shown without the Producers permission as it contains images of family members who have recently passed away.

This 'story' presents evidence of how my family, myself and our peoples have lived in harmony with our sacred ancestral being, Martuwarra since the beginning of time. Sacred ancestral beings with whom we continue to have ceremony, cry, laugh, dance, sing and talk with in our daily lives. The ***River of Life***, Martuwarra is our identity, our spirituality, our Law. It is a law of interdependence for multispecies justice and Indigenous wellbeing. A wisdom circle for planetary health and human survival. With 'friends of Martuwarra', we are in a moment in time in which to right-size the planet and rebalance energy systems through a pluriverse of brave human beings who are coming together to dream a new way of living and being—'*just development on just terms*'.

3.4.2 Bookarrarra—*Dreaming the Time Between Past, Present and Future*

*Bookarrarr*a is a concept from the beginning of time. Please view the film, *Bookarrarra,* at https://vimeo.com/451420394[13]:

> One of the words that we have in our language is a word called *Bookarrarra*. Now *Bookarrarra* means the past, the present and the future, fused into this moment in time in which we as human beings need to be able to respond and react in the protection of Country. So *Bookarrarra* is a very, very important word, and it places us as being Traditional Owners, Indigenous people, who have been here from the beginning of time. And so we have a due diligence to learn from the old stories, to take those stories as First Law stories and to be able to understand that those stories teach us about values, about ethics, about code of conduct, about how to live in a civil society. One of the things that we say as Indigenous people is that

[13] Perdrisat et al. (2021).

> we come from a world of we, not me. And so it's very, very important when we're looking at developing strategies to look at the collective wellbeing of not just Indigenous people, but our fellow Australians and indeed global citizens (Anne Poelina, in Perdrisat, 2021).

3.4.3 Warloongarriy *River Law*

Warloongarriy Law is the Law for the Martuwarra Fitzroy River. It connects all of the Indigenous Nations along the Fitzroy River Catchment, as one society, through the song and ceremony of *Warloongarriy* Law. Please access the film *Warloongarriy* Law at https://vimeo.com/459588320.

> European people can't understand our Law, because they've got a different law. Ours is from *Bookarrarra.* We try to explain these things to them, and they don't know what we're talking about. Because that's from *Bookarrarra.* It's from *Bookarrarra.* But it's different law, different law from White man law. Different. Different altogether (Senior Nyikina Elder of High Degree, Paddy Roe, in *Millenium,* 1992[14]).

In 2016, Traditional Owners expressed a collective vision for the Martuwarra in the Fitzroy River Declaration.[15] Through our collective story and as one society, bound by kinship, obligation and reciprocity, we hold *Warloongarriy* Law.

3.4.4 The Place, the People Our River Country

The Martuwarra (Fitzroy River)[16] is an iconic, heritage listed unregulated river system of global value and significance. We invite you to come, see, feel and hear Martuwarra Country.[17]

Please view the film, *Balkinjirr Poem,* at https://vimeo.com/395462956/20170d66ee.[18]

For Australia's original peoples of the Martuwarra, the River was formed in the beginning of time by Nyikina ancestor, *Woonyoomboo. Woonyoomboo* is the human face of the Martuwarra and in partnership with our sacred ancestral spiritual living beings who created the Martuwarra valley tracts.[19] *Woonyoomboo* was an explorer, map maker and scientist who named the places, animals, birds, fish, plants and living

---

[14] Maybury-Lewis (1992).

[15] Martuwarra Fitzroy River Council (2016).

[16] Allam (2021).

[17] Poelina et al. (2020a).

[18] Poelina and McDuffie (2019a).

[19] The visual content in this story is protected by the Producer Dr. Anne Poelina's Indigenous Cultural and Intellectual Property Rights (ICIP). No visual content is to be shared beyond the scope of this project as the film contains images of people who are recently deceased and cannot be shared without Dr. Poelina's consent.

water systems. These environmental and cultural values are recognised in both the Western Australian Aboriginal Cultural Heritage and National Heritage Listings.

Please view the film *Mardoowarra River of Life* at https://vimeo.com/187590078/7afbbc772d[20]:

> Welcome to the River Country, Mardoowarra, the sacred River of Life. My name is Mardoowarra. When the Europeans came, they called me by another name, Fitzroy River, but I hold to my name which was given to me in the *Bookarrarra*, the beginning of time. I hold my totem, *Yoongoorrookoo*, the Rainbow Serpent who formed the valley tracts as *Woonyoomboo*, the first human being, stood and rode on my back, holding the spears firmly planted in my rainbow skin. As we twisted and turned up in the sky down in the ground together, we carved our way forming the Mardoowarra, singing the *Warloongarriy* River Law song for Country.
>
> I was so happy in 2011, seeing everyone working together, black and white Australians, telling their stories of heritage, culture, and environment. Telling the Australian government to listen to all of the collective wisdom, which helped me to become listed as National Heritage. I hear the voice of Lucy Marshall, Senior Elder, and custodian saying, 'Those people who are playing with nature, they must be stopped'. She's very wise. She knows that together, shoulder to shoulder, we can work together to look after my rights. I am the sacred River of Life. Her sister, Jeannie Warbie, agrees with me and I hear her standing and calling strong, 'No River, No People'. And without our continuing law of relationship between human and non-human beings, there will be no life.
>
> In 2015, Pope Francis issued an encyclical on climate change, in which he says that the cultural and Land rights of Aboriginal peoples are both key factors in the underlying global problems of greed and destruction. And they hold global solutions.
>
> Here in the West Kimberly on the River Country, my peoples are being asked to make way for intensive agricultural and mining projects without consideration for the degradation of nature and their culture or my right to life. Dr. Anne Poelina has written to his holiness, Pope Francis, and her story, Protecting the River of Life, was published by the Vatican, in 2016.
>
> A Tribunal for Nature was held in Brisbane, in October 2016. This citizens' Tribunal has heard cases presented by citizens and Earth lawyers concerned about the destruction of ecosystems and the wider Earth community in Australia. Dr. Poelina brought my case, Mardoowarra versus state of WA and federal government, to the Tribunal to ask the citizens of this court, to recognize me as a living entity with a right to life, like my sister, the Whanganui River in New Zealand.
>
> The Whanganui River has stood strong and with the help of her Indigenous custodians and the strength and wisdom of legal and cultural governance, she now has set international legal precedents across Mother Earth. Her rights in nature gives me hope in human beings, who hold the lives of the other non-human beings, the birds, the trees, the rocks, the insects, and the balance of life in their hands. I call to you to stand with Dr. Poelina as she presents my case to be protected as a sacred river with the right to life for generations to come (Poelina et al. 2016)

3.4.5 Cultural Governance—A Model of Hope and Freedom

In 2018 the Martuwarra Fitzroy River Council ('Council') was established as a legal entity as a 'collective governance model to maintain the spiritual, cultural

[20] Poelina et al. (2016).

and environmental health of the catchment'.[21] The Traditional Owner members of the Council are *Warrwa, Bunuba Dawangarri* Aboriginal Corporation RNTBC, *Walalakoo* Aboriginal Corporation RNTBC, *Yanunijarra* Aboriginal Corporation RNTBC, the Warrwa Registered Native Title Claim Group, *Wilinggin* Aboriginal Corporation and the *Yurriyangem Taam* native title claim group as represented by the Applicant (Parties). As a result, the Martuwarra Council considers the Martuwarra to be communal property, an 'asset in the commons' that belongs to all of us.

The Martuwarra Fitzroy River Council is an alliance of Traditional Owners who stand with *One Mind and One Voice.* A Council of Senior Elders with our younger leaders from Traditional Owner Groups of the King Sound, Fitzroy River, and its Catchment. Our work is grounded in First Law and the guardianship system of rights, responsibility and obligations. Our 'Coalition of Hope' is grounded in '*Martuwarra Fitzroy River, Always Was Always Will Be*', and it must be promoted and protected for the benefit of present and future generations.[22]

As guardians of our living sacred ancestors, we honour six distinct sacred ancestral Rainbow Serpent traditions *Yoongoorookoo, Galbardu, Kurrpurrngu, Mangunampi, Paliyarra* and *Kurungal.* As the Martuwarra Council we maintain and share sophisticated cultural knowledge and practices which empower us as guardians to be the voice of the Living Waters of the Martuwarra Fitzroy River Catchment and its right to live and flow. We stand through kinship, obligation and reciprocity, **Living Waters, Law First**.[23]

3.4.6 Foreseeable Harm Versus Peace with Indigenous People and with Nature

The resource extraction and economic development plans currently being promoted for the Martuwarra Fitzroy River Country and our peoples are complex and confusing, with no investment or opportunity for dialogue with Indigenous people nor with **ALL** citizens who live in the region or who have an interest in its rich heritage. There is no appetite from the Western Australian State government for investment into a Statutory Catchment Management Authority to collectively manage and regulate all development to a high standard from an evidence based, informed consent decision-making position.

This resistance encapsulates the illusion of probity. The pretence is that everything is on the table. We are told it is for the greater good of our nation, but we know it is for a few 'big greedy frogs', who want to, as Mr Brown, Senior Walmajarri Elder states, '*drain the water out, that will kill the culture*'. When it comes to development scenarios planned for Martuwarra Fitzroy River Catchment Estate in reference to

[21] Poelina et al. (2019).

[22] Poelina (2020).

[23] RiverOfLife et al. (2021a).

human rights, climate, water and environmental justice all we can see is foreseeable harm, ecocide and genocide.

> The Kimberley is under attack. We know that there's the potential for coal, uranium, copper, diamonds, bauxite, iron ore, zinc, lead, as well as other precious metals. We know that this industry needs an incredible amount of water. We're really concerned that groundwater would be used and what that would mean for all the pools and the billabongs along the Fitzroy River, particularly in the dry season (Martin Pritchard, Environs Kimberley, in Poelina et al. 2015).[24]

There is little or no investment into understanding or preventing social impact risks to our people and/or the cumulative impact limits required to maintain a clean environment to protect our human and Indigenous specific rights. The commodification of water which prices water as a 'resource' in Australia's south has resulted in catchment scale environmental damage.[25] The Indigenous wisdom and leadership that has emerged in response to the Murray-Darling Basin catastrophe provides 'critical lessons' which we can share and learn from.

Over the past 150 years we have strongly advocated for better Land and river management as well as addressing cumulative threats at a catchment scale.[26] In a time of growing uncertainty of food, water and energy security we need to protect our rivers as the lifeblood and life force of our Country!

Please view the film *Joe Brown: Martuwarra* at https://vimeo.com/546836156/8b3eb7f6e7.[27]

> We sing that story about this River. My favourite story when people ask me, I always sing this song, Martuwarra. It's very important to me, this River. I really love the River. How can government going to try to take over the River? Government didn't born in this river, we born alongside the river. We should be the one that own the River, not government.
>
> It's Law. We got a Law too, and the River got the Law. This River got story, big history. That *Warloongarriy* dream. If River going to go dry that'll kill the culture. We need to fight for this River, not to drain all the water out. Money is nothing, but the life of the River is living there forever (Senior Walmajarri Elder, Mr Joe Brown, 2019).

Through our story we are building a 'Coalition of Hope', with 'Friends of the Martuwarra', such as Dr Michelle Lim.

Please access Michelle Lim's interview at https://vimeo.com/433343821/0023e84b48.[28]

> My name's Michelle Lim... My area is environmental law. What Anne and I have been working on is looking at the intersection between First law, the Law of the River, and State law. First law from the beginning of time is so important and should be the foundation for developing State law. So, by State law, the non-Indigenous law, Commonwealth law. Using that starting point of *Warloongarriy* Law, the River Song, the Law of the River, which

[24] See Poelina et al. (2015)

[25] A significant example is the impact on volume and quality of water in the Murray Darling Basin, which the Australian government has recently tried to repress from a UN book (Brewster 2018).

[26] RiverOfLife et al. (2020b).

[27] RiverOfLife et al. (2020a).

[28] RiverOfLife et al. (2017).

> recognises the River as a living being in its own right, and as the ancestor of people who live in the Martuwarra. So, this understanding of the whole River, the Fitzroy River, Martuwarra as being a Rainbow Snake from the head to the tail. And not only that, that's what it is, and it's what created the people, but that people have an obligation to protect the ancestor, to protect the snake.
>
> And that links the past, the present and the future. How do we create a healthy River from a range of perspectives? So, your social, economic, and environmental, they're all intertwined. So that starting point of how you make the River healthy is defined in a range of different ways. Using the First Law of the River, as that starting point is very helpful in thinking about how can we have a future for the River as a living, being in its own right, and a future for the people of the River. So, a lot of what Anne talks about is how we can envisage the law of the River, which has come from the beginning of time. How do we envisage that for modernity? And going back to the Fitzroy River declaration, which in itself is such a groundbreaking event because it's the first time in Australia that you've got this negotiated instrument, which recognises an ecosystem as a living being in its own right.
>
> And not only have they incorporated the Law of the River in the Fitzroy River Declaration. It's forward-looking as well. It's saying...there's eight points within the Declaration to move towards bringing that First Law into the future, into modernity. And where I come in, I think is in looking at how we can engage and reform existing State law to give effect to some of those points. Something I think that is important and helpful is thinking about the window of time we have that we need to do something now. And in speaking, I'm hearing in my ears again, Anne going, there's this opportunity to prevent a disaster, not just an environmental disaster, not just a social cultural disaster and not just an economic disaster. How we think about the River in a sustainable way and how we put into process, into action, the correct legal frameworks from a state based perspective, which are based on law which has come from so many generations of looking after the River, where we get that interaction between what types of law needs to be in place to give effect to that.[29]

In building our collective consciousness and actions to be creative and adaptive to climate change, we need to ask ourselves individually and collectively, 'Can we have a common and shared future under climate change?' Before we answer these questions, we must first challenge our own practice and redefine our thinking and understanding of 'what is sustainable livelihoods and what is sustainable development'?

How can we use multiple forms of knowledge making and application to better respond and adapt to climate change and planetary wellbeing?[30]

Today, we come together because of the need to think and act differently to ensure our knowledge and collaboration is multidisciplinary and includes the active participation of other actors and stakeholders who have a political and influential role, which impacts on the lives of people and the planet. I believe we can work together collectively to identify the challenges of Land, water, people and the environment in building creative and sustainable solutions to climate change.

> The group that is most often overlooked and yet has probably the greatest wisdom of any group in terms of relation to the environment are the Indigenous communities. And so it's absolutely imperative that these communities be involved in the dialogue and addressing issues like climate change, how to mitigate impacts of other pollutants, and how to work with communities for future development in a way that's sustainable, in a way that can

[29] Michelle Lim (2017).

[30] Redvers et al. (2020a).

be maintained without impacting the environment. And so including these communities is absolutely critical (Dr Jonathan Hook, in Poelina et al. 2015).

This lived experience has generated an extensive body of traditional ecological knowledge production and adaptation to learning how to read the Country, to read and understand nature by looking for the signs up in the sky, down in the ground. This has come about through a deep relationship between human and non-human beings in nature. This system of knowledge must be seen and valued as Indigenous science as framed through First Law.

3.4.7 Where to Next?

The ability to include Indigenous science and First Law into the collective wisdom of our scenario planning and toward modelling for climate change adaptation can eliminate and empower ways of postmodern living. 'Western' ethics have remained largely anthropocentric and indifferent to the fate of the natural world. This is changing slowly as we re-examine the nature of human-Earth relations and begin to build a basis for sustainable life now for the future. It is important to note that sustainable lifeways is not the same as sustainable development. As the latter is increasingly used to promote growth economics with little regard for inherent limitations on ecological systems.

Please access the visual poem *Singing Yoongoorrookoo at* https://vimeo.com/395472554/e52c6ee7d0.

I am *Yoongoorrookoo* the Singing Rainbow Serpent. Traveling high up in the sky and down through the rivers. The air and the sea, the river and the soil. I feel a great sadness now carried by many people. They cry out and ask, 'What is happening in our nation, in our Country, in our home?'

I see below me, floods and fires crisscrossing the Land, big storms and harsh heat. Our knowledge of Country ignored by government and bureaucracy. 'Wake up', I say to you, and hear my belly crawl. Wake up maybe one last time and listen to Bruce Pascoe's call. There's wisdom here, heavily rooted intrinsically between Aboriginal nations. Their Land, living waters, sea and sky. Aboriginal voices being muted in that protection of our rivers, crying out, 'We need to be recognised'.

Defrauded, dis-eased into staying quiet. Now through their mourning, awakening others to their calling. Recognised, reconciled in healing, a united transformation in order to fully nurture the Australian nation. This Australia taken by theft from a lineage of ancestral custodians. It's time to pause and take a deeper breath.

Rivers must have a right to life and their contribution to all other life must be protected. Some are fearful that the humans create their own extinction. I have hope in human beings for living water lives within them too. It's their life, they must save it if they are to continue living on Mother Earth. Mother Earth covered in living waters, cradled beneath the sky. I keep on singing, as I believe a 'Coalition of Hope' is coming.

Indigenous nations believe they have a fiduciary duty as custodians and guardians, legislative river protection acts across the whole Country. This must be done before it's too late. Earth jurisprudence, First Law, law of the Land. This is the cry from the Aboriginal nations of this wide brown Land. This has been the message championed through the rivers of the MDB, rivers have the right to life, they must flow free. This must become a nation song line if the Australian bloodlines are to hold the past, present and future strong. I sing this to you, singing the River Law song for people and Country.[31]

The Martuwarra Council advocates for the political goodwill and research investment required to ensure the concept of 'Just Development' based on Indigenous First Law. Ultimately Traditional Owners' concerns are about property rights, power and values in regard to deeply different ontologies and epistemologies. This has been evidenced in the Martuwarra Council Conservation and Management Plan.[32]

Championing a treaty and reconciliation framework must come to a point of reconciliation in order to affirm 'Black Lives Matter', and they matter as it is time for **justice and equity** to build peace with the First Australians and with nature, especially our rivers. First Law offers a pathway to justice, equity and peace as it incorporates Indigenous Lifeways and Livelihoods. First Law and Traditional Ecological Knowledge (TEK) must be coupled with Western science and actioned through genuine Free Prior and Informed Consent (FPIC). For treaty and reconciliation, identified issues that will need to be fully explored include:

- *Who and what counts and is counted?*
- *How are values assigned?*
- *How do relationships between people and the 'natural' world work to produce value?*
- *How are existing values of the riverine system understood and measured?*
- *Whose laws and values matter?*
- *What impacts and risks are accurately predicted and deemed acceptable?*
- *Who gets to decide? And what kind of 'evidence' is weighed up in the decision-making process?*
- *How and where are decisions made?*
- *Whose visions of the future are being pursued?*

(Poelina, Brueckner, & McDuffie, 2020).[33]

In a time where our Nation has laws, policies, management and regulation collapsing at every level it is time to build a vision which unites ALL Australians. Climate investment funds must be committed and invested into better understanding the sciences, the industry and the political challenges and solutions to adapt and respond to the survival of humanity and the planet.

This type of investment must be directed toward the design and situational context in order to support the collaboration of regional governance frameworks, which shifts the balance of power to local people and stakeholders who need to build a vision and a collective and common future together. We need to develop a unity pathway,

[31] Poelina and McDuffie (2019b).

[32] RiverOfLife et al. (2020d).

[33] Poelina et al. (2020b), p. 8.

share information and have informed decision-making through regional governance approaches.

The First Australians are extending their gift of wisdom, knowledge and practice, to assist in nation building, healing and reconciliation. Who knows in the circle of time we may one day achieve a 'Just Energy Transition' and be ready for a 'Just Republic'?

> We can run the Country. We know what the rules are. We never forget. Together. Together shoulder to shoulder. We know what's right and what's wrong. Sorry about that, but we still got our culture. We still got our role. We still got a role to play (Lucy Marshall, in Poelina et al. 2015).

These words are coming as a gift to humanity; it is time to stop 'othering' Indigenous people and our ancient wisdom, which is so necessary to planetary and multispecies wellbeing. This ancient wisdom is coming as a gift from our peoples. It is about strengthening the opportunities for the 'forever industries'.[34] We are worried about our Rivers as Living Water Law First, as Rivers are the lifeblood, our lifeways and our sustainable livelihoods and economies of our Country.

> If we are to survive, then we have got to listen to Indigenous peoples, and we've got to build those links between non-native and native communities and move forward as partners and in partnership of equals. And coming to the table, doesn't mean simply sharing ideas, which is a very important part, it means being part of the decision-making process. Not simply being informed after the fact, but being part of determining the steps that are taken forward and being true equals in that process.
>
> We're at a tipping point. And unless we take action now, unless we are forceful emotionally, and perhaps in written documents and video statements and in relationship building with governmental entities and scientists. Unless we take those steps now, this tipping point means that if it tips too far, we won't be able to go back (Dr Jonathan Hook, in Poelina et al. 2015).

By reframing and building collective wisdom, by opening our minds, we can start to shape not only what we 'dream' future laws to be, but what the law can be now. Through our collaboration and stories there is an emergence of research and dialogue which starts to redefine the law around **existing rights of justice and equity**.[35]

Please access the film *Martuwarra River of Life at* https://vimeo.com/533047074/87705efc9e.[36]

We have started a conversation for how to build peace with Indigenous Australians and with our Nation; it will move in the circle of time. We share our stories of First Law, Law of the Land so we can better understand how we, as human beings, can once again start to live in harmony with each other and with our non-human families and defend our amazing planet, Mother Earth, from climate chaos and destruction. Otherwise, ***Mother Earth will be lonely without the vibrations of human beings***!

---

[34] See Australian Conservation Foundation (2021)

[35] RiverOfLife et al. (2020c).

[36] RiverOfLife et al. (2021b).

3.5 Ross (Timmulba) Williams

The Journey of One, the Journey of Many

Biography

My name is Ross Williams—traditional name is Timmulba (Lightning) and I am a proud Bindal person of Townsville and Burdekin regions on my father's side and on my mother's side connected to the Islands and peoples of Erub and Mer in the Torres Straits.

I have over 40 years' experience working with traditional owner groups, Elders and Leaders, in government roles and non-government organisations on Aboriginal and Torres Strait Islander environmental, social, cultural, economic and planning matters. I have been working as a freelance researcher and evaluation consultant over the last seven years providing specialist advice to projects and programs across Australia in the social determinate's areas and the cultural heritage and environmental fields.

Previously I have worked for the Queensland Environmental Protection Agency and the Great Barrier Reef Marine Park Authority and recently, I have led the work on the evaluation of the Cape York Peninsula Aboriginal Land Joint Management Program, the National Park Ranger joint management program and facilitated the state-wide First Nations futures programs for the Great Barrier Reef Foundation.

3.5.1 Learning the Law of the Land

Walking for the first of many times with my father and my uncles as we went on a hunt for food, would teach me many techniques and cultural values that would guide and teach me the values of the environment that I later learnt were activities carried out over thousands of generations by my peoples. At the age of five it was simply fun, the fun of going bush, the fun of spending time with my father, uncles and my Elders reading the bush by tracking animals, looking for signs, understanding its offerings and understanding the cultural and spiritual side of what I was doing.

Growing up through my teenage years, the experiences of traveling to and through the bush and various landscapes hunting and gathering, as I did as a young boy, continued to be exciting and rewarding activities, but this time I was elevated to take on the added responsibilities of not just a hunter, but in part, a provider. This was done with friends and cousins looking for food, preparing it and cooking for the family tables and gatherings. Unconsciously I continued to hunt fish and gather using techniques and knowledge passed onto me and learnt through continuous practices, observations and self-learnings from and of the bush, rivers and sea environments, through the many hunting and gathering activities.

Practices of using the sun and moon phases, weather activities, seasonal variations and signs like flowering and fruiting plants, Land animals, bird movements, sounds and songs, animal prints and droppings, smells, wind movements and the many other signs. The practice of the flowering wattles telling of the mullet runs; moths, butterflies, bats, bees, ants, lizards and snakes and many other animal movements were all signs that I learnt without fully understanding the interaction but knowing that each of these activities were signals. I learnt about fungi, mosses, ground covers, seaweeds and seagrasses and much more, all knowledge not just for survival if ever needed, but what each animal depended on for their sustenance and survival as well.

This all coincided with the variation in seasons and all the subtleness of how animals and plants needed these changes to trigger the need to feed and breed. I watched this and learnt from a variety of teachers and put it into practice every day as a fun thing to do. Tracking of animals was one of my favourite activities as a child right through to now: to see which animal made which tracks and tracking their movements in and through the bush and the different landscapes, vegetation types, open plains and waterways, coastal Lands and seascapes.

My appetite for knowledge saw me wanting to teach young people my skills and pursue a career in the Land and cultural management in the hope that I would have further access to Elders and knowledge holders of culture and cultural practices. Teaching young people was and is a passion and I knew I would pursue roles that combined my love of learning about the environment and Aboriginal people and Torres Strait Islanders and the synergies between both.

Teaching and telling stories, doing cultural tours, was an overly exciting period, so much so that I applied for a role in the Queensland government as an Archaeological Ranger. This allowed me to do what I loved to do, teaching cultural activities, and sharing and applying my knowledge and skills. Aboriginal and Torres Strait Islander cultural site identification, protection and management added to the dimensions of what I thought I knew from a cultural perspective. It created a new world of learning, particularly about landscapes and how cultural sites are different and how these sites are intrinsically connected to the peoples of the areas, all of which told stories. The difficult part was piecing together the intricacies of peoples, laws and places through Land laws and cultural lore and practices so I could better understand nature and peoples' relations to their Lands, water, flora, fauna, sky and each other.

Spending much of my time as physically possible with and around peoples who were the story holders, the holders of law, cultural storytellers, the holder and practitioners of songlines, sacred and secret knowledge holders, clan knowledge holders and language keepers and speakers, the teachers both men and women, teachers for and of Country in its holistic form, was the essence of my learnings.

My overwhelming desire to learn was more about my search for my own cultural identity in the fragments of my own culture. It was a search for meaning within a very hostile existence and the survival against colonial oppression. The most valuable lessons were to live and learn through practices and teachings of my peoples from their lived experiences across the state and across Australia.

3.5.2 Dispossession and Its Continuing Harm

The journeys of learning were spent in the landscapes with peoples across parts of this continent and in Canada with the Mohawk, Haida Gwaii and Inuit peoples, learning and experiencing First Nations peoples' applied knowledge and practices. This, I was to learn, was within the web of intergenerational traumas and struggles while holding on to their laws of the Lands and waters, to maintain and sustain oneself and one's peoples in the fragmented landscape.

These experiences and learning have taught me that dispossession of people's Lands was by force, and an extremely aggressive and pervasive march to force the disconnect of First Nations peoples from their homelands and waters. Despite spending valuable time with First Nations peoples in the remote regions of this Country hunting, gathering and enjoying Country through their eyes, the Land still yearned for healing to be done so that it can come back to life and bring the many plants and animals with it. The Elders always spoke of the Country having a memory that goes back a long way and will come back to how it was before.

The old men would, year after year, talk of the Country needing burning to bring back life, but I really did not know what that meant until a couple of old men a few times would burn Country and then take off in a great hurry. I learnt they did not get the approvals from National Parks or landholders, but later I would find out that they knew exactly what they were doing, when, where and why without harm.

The permission for the burns was given by the Land; and not needed from white man as they would say, despite playing in the back of their minds that they, if caught, could be prosecuted, hence why we did not hang around for too long. The old men would show me and others the landscape they would burn, or intended to burn, and define that landscape from the grasses, plants, trees, animals, winds, seasons, the soils and type of fires needed and why. They would teach us how to read the Country and what habitat and vegetation types would need burning and how that fire, if done right, would self-extinguish using natures landscape itself.

> If it is a good fire the wind will dance with that fire, if it is a bad fire, it will be loud and angry. I'm giving this Country good fire (Elder, Cape York)

They would also explain the plants and weeds that should not be in that landscape, and how some of those plants were poison to Country and to the native animals and livestock. They would say that if we do not control these poison plants the Country would be further destroyed, and the Country would become sick.

Cattle were often discussed as a destructive animal, not to mention, wild horses, pigs, goats, dogs, etc., but cattle were not seen in the same destructive vein as the other introduced species as I later learnt that cattle were the reasons for peoples to stay and move around on Country as stockmen, roustabouts and domestics, a lifeline to cultural connection and the support to continue many of their practices.

3.5.3 Colonial Law Inconsistent with First Law

Cultural observances and practices were continually conducted in a way that was subtle in nature, natural in its flow, with seamless transitions and interactions. Obligations to nature and therefore laws of the Land were presented by and from the Lands. What is meant by that is nature provides you with signs and tells you when and where it is the right time to interact and or partake. Laws of obligation compel that you are not to take more than what was needed and that you would express your thanks for those gifts which would be returned over your lifetime.

What did not become obvious straight away was that peoples could see into and from the landscapes, watching the activities, watching the Lands, waters, plants and animals do things in a transfixed and harmonious dance with each other, and that they themselves as Aboriginal peoples are part of that movement. From the time of the year, subtle movement in seasons to movements of the animals, to the transition of the plants to the colours of the skies are all moments and movements.

Elders and holders of knowledge always spoke of transforming with your environment and adapting to the songs and teaching of our spirits. They spoke of Earth as our ancestors which gives life provides for the needs of life and that when it is time, we go back to the Earth to join our ancestors. They spoke of the spirits in the trees, rivers, rocks, animals and the stars, all around us taking up many different forms to once again give and support life, the Land is our teacher. To cause harm to our ancestral homelands is to cause harm to us all and the generations to come.

Looking after Land, looking after Country was described as not only a responsibility but a sacred duty to the Land and the law in those Lands. When describing Lands, it means, all things living on, or fixed, moving on, or through, under or over including waters and air. The old peoples told of caring for Country as a doing word and not just saying words, measuring their words by what they did. They are speaking of white man's way of looking after Country. It was sometimes described as the 'white way' and not the right way or the 'true way'.

3.5.4 Earth Law as a Basis for Protecting Aboriginal Peoples' Rights

The competing nature and changing nature of Land use is still difficult for Aboriginal peoples to understand, not to mention the laws that continue to change to protect the ways of the white peoples. Aboriginal peoples know and interact with nature as fixed laws which can never be changed or altered, but it is us as humans that must adapt to nature's needs.

> My Country gave me life, helped look after me and when it is time, I will go back to Country (Inuit Leader)

The old peoples showed their Country through a cultural landscape lens and would share the many maps in their minds of their traditional Lands. They would not only translate the landscapes, but also what was in the landscape at any given moment and time. The mind maps, I was to find out, consisted of a survival map, where to find water even in the driest of times, foods and medicines. Then there were the walking tracks and trails that would get you to and from places, there were markers for different survival needs and there were cultural markers for activities.

Country also contains many sacred places and sites, art sites and the many mosaics of important locations. Many of these places cannot be told to others despite some of these places succumbing to destruction either unwittingly or through wilful and deliberate ignorance. These sites underpin story places, cultural practices and the stories of tens of thousands of years from the time of the ancestral Dreamings, to becoming humans on the continent, to the transition to the present and modern humans.

The old and wise Aboriginal and Torres Strait Islander peoples spoke of their need for adaptation to a change in landscapes particularly since European arrival and the destruction, use and abuse of their environment and their homelands. They talk of the seasons changing, plants and animals moving further away from Country and other signs that have come to be known and referred to as climate change.

They speak of the devastation of mass Land clearing on their Country, they talk of the overfishing, the use of long nets, the indiscriminate impact on the animals and their habitats and the flow-on effect of the impacts on their lives, their cultures, the social, economic and psychological impacts, and the need to survive.

The old peoples often spoke of the white man's laws that stop them from fishing, hunting and gathering their own foods and medicines.

> Their laws are destroying us, this white man's laws are not right, the white man's law keeps changing, but our laws stay the same (Cape York Elder)

What I have learnt so far is that our Lands and environment is First Law. For our peoples it is a fixed Law that governs who we are as a people and underpins our very existence. We learn from our Lands and our environment; it teaches us to live within the boundary of Earth laws and rules. If we do not listen and learn from the Earth and the oldest continuous culture, we as humanity will succumb to Earth's laws and therefore cease to exist.

3.6 Chels Marshall

Energy, Salty Water and Planetary Cycles

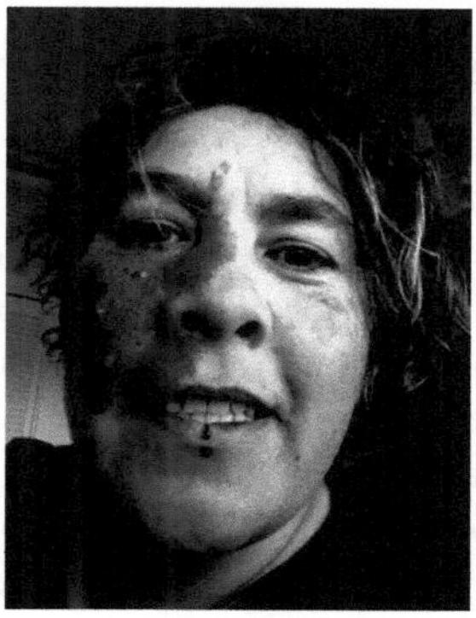

Biography

Gagaal (Ocean) is my Gumbaynggirr Totem, it is the thing that defines and identifies me. My family totem is the Red Bass, a fish that thrives and cycles through this medium. Through kinship I have cousins who are sharks and ancestors and family who are whales and dolphins. Everything in my cultural teaching and upbringing is about the ocean, the cycles, seasons, the interconnections, its moods, its importance and the laws attached to it.

My undergraduate university studies, my work and career, my Masters Thesis, my professional life, my art, my research, my PhD, my teaching, my lecturing, my academic writing, my weekend and down time is Gagaal derived. It cools me down, like it does for the planet. Am I obsessed? Probably yes, its health and protection are my inherited responsibility, it is alive, it keeps me alive, alive in all forms, its wellbeing is my wellbeing, and it is a part of me as I am a part of it.

To understand the context in which the Gumbaynggirr people utilised the landscape, one must recognise Gumbaynggirr as a distinct cultural group (own stories, language, songs, etc.). The complexity of the language developed from the landscape over thousands of years for how we lived and continue to live and interact with the natural environment. Ultimately, it is essential to value how language and Land are connected and understand the context of how places are created and given perspective and meaning.

This is my homeland, this is jagun and bari. This is where I come from. This is my landscape, my part that touches this vast and magnificent Pacific Ocean. This is my association to this part of Country. It extends from the Clarence River to the Nambucca River and Yarrabiny Mountains in the south. This coastline has cultural meaning, and the meaning extends from what it was prior to European invasion. Understanding the names and meanings of places in Gumbaynggirr Country and our connection to landscape creation provides insight into the balanced existence and significance of culture and spirituality in the sustainability of healthy, functioning marine and terrestrial ecosystems.

3.6.1 Recognising Past Injustices and Correcting Falsehoods

I have come through a period of schooling in Australia where history began in 1788. When Captain Cook 'discovered' Australia and the British colonisation founded a nation. The reference to First Nations peoples, not only here in Australia but the whole world was a negative description, perceived as 'noble savages' or 'a backward race'. My memories of kindergarten still ring through like yesterday, the only Aboriginal kid, belittled in front of my class by my teacher when, in show and tell, I told them of the giant golden kangaroo (Nunguu Miirlarl) that hopped over the Gumbaynggirr landscape and rests as a mountain for all to see a reminder about greed and the sinister act of killing what you don't know. My teacher quickly dismissed this, saying 'there were no giant animals in Australia' and that it is wrong to make up stories—how wrong she was. Through my family's experiences, I received the other side of this skewed history and the cognitive manipulation attached to the education system at that time. I understand the intent of the strategies in colonisation, I comprehend how our ancestors fought to protect and conserve our beautiful Country then, as they still do today.

I understand that bari (Country) has laws and these were and continue to be broken time after time by pressures and mindset of an industrial society.

Rewriting history from Indigenous perspectives is a part of the paradigm shift. Indigenous perspectives provide balance to historic and contemporary research, writings and design. It gives insight to different lenses and perspectives of various issues, coming from different worldviews in culturally appropriate ways. This is also the case with law and management of 'Country'.

I spent all my childhood, teenage years and adult life growing up on Country and not only listening to, but living and experiencing the knowledges of culture and environment, not only the law of Gumbaynggirr bari (landscapes/Country) but also from other parts of Australia: the connective thread is derived from respect, respect for all living entities and living within our means. The gradual understanding and comprehension of 'Dreamtime, stories and Songlines' or creation and the laws of wajarr (Earth) and bari (Country) has shifted my whole perspective on the environment, living and life. From a young age, the understandings of interactions between humans and Earth cycles and processes are very important. More important is your place in Country and within the natural cycles of Country. The associated behaviours and laws then also enhanced my understanding of the right to exist in equity with the landscape, the species within, and respect for the natural cyclic functions of life and renewal.

I am a true believer of the notion 'look after Country and it will look after you'. At the moment I am angry and in pain as is Country. The Nambucca Bindary (river) is one of the main sustenance areas for our food. It has a mouth that has smashed and destroyed many timber and steel ships. Jagun's steep curves and peaks, dense rainforest gullies and strong mountains deterred the European settler for a very long time. The scratches and cuts from our plants and rocks too painful for soft strange flesh. These bari variables held off the colonisers for a very long time in comparison with other places on the east coast impact area. We are still here, so is Country and, and so are our laws. Like the ocean, I am sometimes angry.

My anger at the moment derives from the continuing colonisation and the destruction of our native forests, every day families of trees are killed, I have to listen to the screams of the trees, slaughtered and left bare for all to see, the logging trucks parade along the highway with the carcass stacked, almost like a trophy, it is sickening. It's these families of trees that provide our breath, sustain our atmosphere, they clean and filter water and ensure its health when it moves and merges through Country, nourishing mountains, underground life and entering the sea.

From my parents, grandmother, Aunts and Uncles and family, I really began to understand the significance of 'creation stories' and the laws of bari, to realise that I should record these stories, experiences and knowledges as a historical record for the future generations of my family and to help the wider community understand the experiences and perspectives of Aboriginal people and our knowledge of environmental functions. Not only documenting our knowledge of natural resources and their appropriate management but ensuring generational knowledge transfer took place on Country in practice. The importance of Indigenous knowledge transfer, maintenance of cultural practice, access to Country and the relationship between wellbeing and ecosystem health is extremely important for our health and survival.

3.6.2 Protecting Key Ecological Assets Is an Ancient Practice

Understanding the places you were not to go and the attached laws, many of these it turns out are breeding or spawning grounds or areas where species need reprieve. Our Giidan (moon story) shows this distinctively and strictly, where only certain sections of people at particular times were able to access the island (now known as Mutton Bird Island, Coffs Harbour). This area is a breeding site for mutton birds and lobster and as you could imagine, without law these resources would diminish. Such places are the original form and notion of protected areas. These teachings were the catalyst for my life, as I grew older, especially when I started university studying natural resource management and wildlife ecology and working as a National Park protected area manager (Ranger). The similarities in cultural species management, habitat management and significance of places on the landscape such as headlands, wetlands and water holes are very comparable to the values placed by Western philosophies in protected area management. A key difference is the superimposed dominant paradigm of colonial European legislations and dominating legal systems that in many cases smother and confine the existing Indigenous systems and laws.

The other is the ideology attached to a protected area as a clearly defined geographical space dedicated and managed through legal or other effective means to achieve long-term conservation of nature, ecosystem services and cultural values (IUCN definition 2008).[37] The foundations of these "protected areas are with Western scientific assessment and Western values". One could argue that from an Indigenous perspective this 'geographical space' is essentially the whole of Australia or what natural areas are left and the 'other means' is the Aboriginal Law attached to these places.

3.6.3 *Indigenous Scientific Knowledge Can Humanise the Impacts of Environmental Harm and Help in Recovery*

One area where the similarity deviates and currently at the forefront of sustainability crisis today is large scale natural resource extraction and capitalist economies attached to these extractive industries, especially where they exist on significant Aboriginal Lands or significant natural areas.

My doctorate aimed to advance our understanding of a key issue in resource management in a multi-cultural context—what are the most effective strategies for realising the benefits of Indigenous approaches to sustainable resource use in the era of climate change? To fully understand this issue, I set out to examine the relationships of diverse forms of Indigenous knowledge to each other, and to global Western scientific approaches, either in partnered co-management or distinctively, comparing Indigenous Australian and Pacific Islander environmental knowledge and management for practical environmental and cultural resilience returns/benefits. This thesis also aimed to decolonise the academic expectation when writing and researching Indigenous topics from Indigenous researchers. The research was undertaken with creative elements to enhance the understanding of the intangible components of culture and relationships that really have no justice applied when writing about them with Western methodology and English language.

Our knowledge contributes to climate science by offering observations and interpretations at a much finer spatial scale with considerable temporal depth and by highlighting elements that may not be considered by climate scientists. It also humanises climate-related issues such as sea level rise, food security and cultural sustainability.

The Pacific Ocean supports an array of ocean-based economies and global food resources. It is essentially the driving force of the Earth's climate and the storeroom of complex ecosystems and marine biodiversity. It is the lungs of the planet, a diverse space that has acted as a sentinel to the many species that have evolved in relative isolation. Climate change impacts are happening now in the Pacific due to its geographic location in vulnerable environments (i.e. coastlines, islands). It is now more than ever time for that paradigm shift.

---

[37] IUCN. *Protected Areas*. Available at: https://www.iucn.org/theme/protected-areas/about.

From an Indigenous perspective, the climate change space and discussions are currently highly dominated by Western science and politics. Unfortunately, the progress in understanding Indigenous culture and cultural needs has not advanced to a point where social-ecological knowledge and primacy in ontological theory or rationale has been injected into the debate. One prime example is the use of traditional seasonal cycles and cultural calendars. The movement away from the Northern Hemisphere's four-season calendar and cycle may assist in adaptation. Its replacement with our knowledge and calendars would be better suited to understand the fluctuations and changes in seasonal variations and climatic cycles along with associated changes to plant and animal variations and adaptations in the equatorial region. It also is an environmental monitoring device. By acknowledging the seasonal variations of an equatorial location, Indigenous interpretations of weather, climate and species observations provide a deeper understanding of seasonal climatic changes and are better suited over the Northern Hemisphere's four-season variation.

Changes to knowledge and understanding require participation in practice and observation of transformation, essential components to Indigenous knowledge systems when applied to cultural landscape connection and continuation. The issues of climate change, national adaptations and resource management need to have a space to consider and discuss the impacts to cultural identity and the integrity of cultural landscapes for Indigenous people. Effective adaptation planning requires access to the best available knowledge, whatever its source. In the face of climate change, where risks and impacts remain uncertain and unpredictable, there is a growing need for an expansion of ideology that directs policies and actions that in turn foster the co-production of new knowledge sets.

Giingan.gundi maangun bindaala: Juungamala ngiyambaygu

(Let's Build a Law/Lore Belonging to Peace: Let's Set Things Right, For All of Us)

The following original story was told to me and my cousins as children. This story was conveyed by my grandmother's brother Uncle Harry Buchanan and reprinted by the Muurrabay Language Centre in 2015. It is the story of Guruja (the whale), the Dungirr gagu (koala brothers) and Baligin (the quoll). It is a continuing epic second component to the Making of the Sea, a five-part series. This story is interpreted and written with my kin sister Shar Smith (2019).

> It was an act of violence against the sacredness of life and Country that resulted in the two Goanna Sisters making the sea. The Land became flooded and the people who were far out on the ocean fishing became cut off from their homeland. They took refuge on a hilltop and asked the Koala Brothers if they could use their intestines to make a bridge back to their homeland. All the people were on the bridge making their way back when the mischievous Baligin (eastern quoll) filled them with fear by making the waves bigger and threatening to chop down the bridge. He continued his mischief by calling in the huge sea creature, Guruja, the whale. However, Guruja could see the people were afraid and reassured them he was there to help them. Guruja carried in his huge heart much love and respect for all life, for life is sacred. He started singing and his song went straight into the hearts of the people, so they were then filled with the same love and respect. The people felt strong, relaxed, encouraged and continued on their way to their drastically changed jagun (landscape). They knew they

> would need to listen to Bari (Country) to hear the new songs and to see the new dances. They would have new responsibilities and new relationships. They would need to make new agreements to be part of the continuation in the sacredness and holisticness of all life, to build again the law belonging to place and peace.

The story the Making of Gaagal (The Sea) has two main female characters, the Goanna Sisters; they are responsible for making the ocean, the coastline and the north and south winds. They now sit in the sky as part of the Seven Sisters Song Line the star constellation (the Pleiades). They remind us of the role females have in maintaining ocean lore and ceremony and the reasons women have integrated and integral roles in the management of marine environments and the protection and associated responsibilities of looking after our Gumbaynggirr totem, the ocean. They also remind us of climate change. The other components of the story tell of the last sea level rise, the intensity of storms and the changes of the Land and seascape. It reminds and warns us of the fear and hysteria that could happen. It tells us of the whales that started their migrations up the east coast and the love and happiness they brought with them as they still do today. This story is a reminder, a warning and a solution to the consequences of climate change and sea level rise.

This application of holistic Indigenous management contrasts with models built on Western ideology in both science and culture, where science tends to focus on reductionist explanations and is accompanied by a worldview that isolates and separates humans from and above the natural world.

I feel that if the acceptance and application of our knowledge is not given a place or as ‘recognised entity’ in a toolbox of applications, it will always be an add on or novelty for Western science and scientists. It will also always be deconstructed, compartmentalised and used without its complete, holistic philosophy.

This, in reality, poses obstacles at the institutional and policy levels when applying its validity. There is no doubt that Indigenous knowledge contributions to conservation and the sustainable use of biodiversity have benefited the ideologies and perspectives of both Indigenous and non-Indigenous peoples. Acknowledgement of ‘another science’ flowing onto species, habitats, ecosystems and interactive biosphere dynamics, management and conservation based on environmental–human connectivity or eco-centric mindset, have a place in resilience and adaptation to human-induced climate change.

We currently exist in a dominant paradigm where we find rightness in short-term thinking and compromise in short-term gain and solutions in band-aid methodologies. As humans with the inability to accept and execute change in a closed technological society. I cannot help but wonder if the resistance to let go of these privileged, comfortable positions is because everything else seems primitive, romantic or too big of a change in socio-political engineering.

Our Knowledges, laws and systems that engage in natural systems and species equity, sharing and true sustainability as a foundational construct would be a very compromising move for a society that prides itself on the industrialism of productivity imposed by the interests of capital and private profit. If this way of existing and consciousness does not change and the laws of the Earth continue to be ignored, our mother will get angrier, and we collectively will endure the ramifications of this disrespect and ignorance.

3.7 Tyson Yunkaporta

The Basic Physics of First Law

Biography

Tyson Yunkaporta is an Aboriginal academic and traditional wood carver, author of *Sand Talk: How Indigenous Thinking Can Save the World*[38] and founder of the Indigenous Knowledge Systems Lab at Deakin University. He holds a doctorate in education and conducts multidisciplinary research projects encompassing cognition, complexity science, governance, economics, geo-politics and cybernetics.

3.7.1 My Identity

I am a boy belonging to the Apalech Clan from Western Cape York, living within the Law of my own clan but also the **greater continental common Law that exists in an ancient network of Songlines and ceremony sites all over Australia**. I'm still a boy at 48 because a swimming pool was built on top of the initiation site I should have gone through to become a man decades ago, although when I am able to take a couple of months off work and away from my duties as a father of young children, I may still 'go through the Law' and become initiated anywhere on this continent and its islands; as my Dad Kenlock tells me, 'Bora is Bora, same Law everywhere'. I

[38] Yunkaporta (2019).

have begun the preparatory stages of this initiation process in recent years, although this has been disrupted by the COVID-19 pandemic.

I have a lot of affiliations all over the continent, through the informal adoptions that occur between Aboriginal people when you live and work on 'other Country', when you are brought into relation with that community for the duration of your stay. This regulates your behaviour and ensures you come under the Law of each place while you are there. Often this occurs even with non-Indigenous visitors who have the capacity to understand and meet the obligations that come with this relationship.

However, full customary adoption is a very different process, occurring for Indigenous people who have lost family, in which the adoptee completely takes on the genealogies of their adopted family and forgo former affiliations and claims. This is one of the few aspects of our Law that is recognised under the law of the colony and crown, through the Mabo case in which Eddie Mabo's adoptive link to his Land was upheld in court. This is the same Law under which I am adopted into my clan. Although I am often under pressure by settlers to identify with my previous Aboriginal lineage for administrative purposes, I stand by our Law no matter what.

3.7.2 Role

As the youngest sibling in our family, I have limited status in terms of speaking for the Law. However, I do have the cultural role of a wood carver and am able to make Yuk Puuyngk, which are Law sticks. These can be smaller message sticks, roughly improvised markers of claims, ceremonial objects or large fighting clubs. They may be stuck in the ground to assert custodial authority of places and resources, by the people who speak for those things in each place. Yuk Puuyngk also carry the Law of story places, with the lore of those places encoded as expressions of First Law in images, songs and narratives.

As I also carry the role of translating basic cultural concepts for outsiders, my practice is to make carvings that contain Indigenous knowledge and then translate parts of those knowledges (that are appropriate to share) into English speech and print. My ability to perceive and interpret the complexities of contemporary global systems through the lens of traditional knowledge and Law means that I am often engaged with finding the 'story' of emerging phenomena through an Indigenous method of inquiry, so that these things can be understood and classified in our lore. It is a slow process, and my contribution is only a small part of that business, which can take decades and involves many people yarning and doing ceremony. This is the same process of Law that has resulted in Dreamings for tobacco, steel, water buffalo, cat, dog and pig.

As part of this traditional process of inquiry in my cultural role, I have worked to create interpretations back and forth between two worlds of jurisprudence. The most difficult part of this is facilitating settler understanding of basic principles of Aboriginal Law. **Many can understand the concept of lore, which is cultural expression arising from the Law of the Land, but most have trouble grasping**

the nature of the concept I have translated as First Law. Many more still get the concepts of lore and Law confused, as they are inextricably linked together and interrelated. My way of approaching this interpreting process has been to begin at the most basic foundation of the Law of the Land as an observable phenomenon that communicates clear limits as to what can be done on Country. The nearest settler equivalent of this knowledge is the discipline of physics, so I begin at the kindergarten level of our Law by engaging with the laws of thermodynamics.

3.7.3 First and Second Laws of Thermodynamics

The first law of thermodynamics correlates with our First Law in that nothing is created or destroyed, but just transforms and moves across systems. One system's entropy is another system's lunch, so that creation is structured in closed loops whereby nothing is wasted, and everything is distributed, self-sustaining, self-governing and interconnected in ways that make natural systems sentient. This kind of dynamic self-organisation in systems is known in contemporary science as autopoiesis. Our traditional societies, economies and governance are also patterned on the physics of these Land-based systems, through totemic systems that inform kinship relations.

The second law of thermodynamics correlates with the law of second peoples (settlers) as it is based on a theoretical notion of closed systems, existing completely within an enclosure that prevents interaction with other systems. If such a vacuum were possible (and physicists say it is not), then the complexity of the system within the enclosure would break down, and this is what physicists explain as the reason for 'the arrow of time', which is the way linear time always progresses forward. While a true vacuum is impossible, the globalising cultures that live under this law and within this arrow of time do create enclosures with membranes that are far less permeable than those of the Land and the people of the Land. This increases entropy, which is the breaking down of complexity in systems. It is the unravelling of creation.

This law of physics is mirrored in the property laws of second peoples, particularly in relation to Land as capital. All Land is divided into parcels that are enclosed by boundaries signalling ownership. The free movement of human and non-human agents (including animals, winds, waters and plants) is inhibited, and the exchange of energy and information (spirit) is stifled across entire bioregions. Humans as a custodial species are denied access to this Land to care for it. This is because an asset can only be priced in the law and economy of second peoples if it is limitable and excludable, so access must be limited and enforced with the threat of violence. The choice of who is granted access to Land is determined by a caste system that is organised by zoning laws and many other laws that create structural inequality.

This caste system is essential for a growth-based economic system to function, as an economy cannot grow unless demand exceeds supply, meaning there must always be more people needing goods and services than what is available. This is called the Economic Problem. It requires that laws uphold a social caste system that makes commodities and capital limitable and excludable to ever increasing numbers of people in the lower castes. In this way, a system of enclosures inhibiting the regenerative process of the first law of thermodynamics in the landscape must be upheld in order for the economy to function.

This system requires inequality and exponential extraction of resources and energy from Land and communities. It also needs to outsource the entropy (destructive violence, toxic waste, depleted soils and more) of the extractive system to zones occupied by people from the lower castes and occupied by non-human beings (rivers, species, climates, soils). These damaged ones are referred to as externalities.

3.7.4 Serpent Lore

In seeking the foundational story of this second law, I found the myth of the Ouroboros. This is the serpent from the Northern Hemisphere, a creator being that is expressed in different forms in every culture. I recognise the serpent as the entity that facilitates our continental common Law on this continent and probably once carried that same common Law of the Land all over the world. However, the civilising myth of the Ouroboros bent that serpent around and made it eat its own tail. It is regarded as a symbol of infinity, but through the lens of Aboriginal Law this can only be seen as a curse, as that snake will not continue forever if it is eating itself. It can only die.

I have begun the work of applying our First Law to undoing this curse. One aspect of this was carving a Law stick with the Ouroboros on it, but wrapped around the 3D knob of the stick. The image was etched deep in the wood, with the tail not quite touching the mouth of the serpent. Dingo and moon story of endless cycles of time was also carved alongside it. The stick is then rolled around the perimeter of a massive circle of clay, producing an image in relief of an endless line of creation serpents. Instead of an entropic enclosure under the second law of thermodynamics, this creates a closed loop of limitlessly regenerative energy and matter, shifting time into the first law of thermodynamics rather than the second.

But I was not the first to suggest this model of time and physics. In Western science, the idea of what has come to be known as the Laws of Thermodynamics was formulated over a period of time by many mathematicians and physicists. By the nineteenth century, among those whose ideas most explicitly related to the laws of thermodynamics, was Rudolf Clausius, who in 1850, posited cyclic thermodynamic processes and the existence of a particular function of state of the system or entropy. Another scientist whose work contributed to these notions was William Rankine.[39]

In thinking about what were previously considered to be controversial ideas, such as Darwin's theory of natural selection, but which are now the accepted norm, perhaps the theory of the first law of thermodynamics as an appropriate model of time also deserves the same respect. The views of these early scientists, mathematicians and

[39] William John Macquorn Rankine (5 July 1820–24 December 1872) was a Scottish mechanical engineer.

other thinkers certainly have more sway than a black boy with a stick, making pictures in clay!

3.7.5 Uncertainty

Applying First Law to physics does require a restructuring of many disciplines though. In particular, it resolves the issues of observer effects and the uncertainty principle in research. The uncertainty principle holds that the act of observing or measuring a speck changes its behaviour and state. So if you are observing its velocity it becomes a wave, and if you are observing its location it becomes a particle. In all areas of scientific inquiry, this scales up to the phenomenon of observer effect, which is understood as the problem of systems changing in response to the scientist's act of observing them.

The story I found for this one was the famous thought experiment of Schrödinger's Cat, in which you imagine a poisoned cat in a box. You can't see the cat but must decide whether it is alive or dead. The conclusion is that you open the box, and the act of seeing a dead cat makes the cat dead, while the act of seeing it living makes it alive. While the box remains closed, it is both alive and dead at the same time!

I consulted a Gamilaroi mathematician, Rick Shaw, to design a story for this which would undo the curse of that entropic enclosure, that second law cat box (and maybe put the spirit of that cat to rest). What we came up with was Schrödinger's Wombat.

So, a wombat is in a hollow log, and we have to decide whether it is alive or dead. However, because the log is not an enclosed system, we are aware of the thousands of exchanges of energy, matter and information between the log and the surrounding Country. We see what the insects are doing, the fungi on the log and surrounding trees, the season and knowledge of how the wombat behaves at that time. We see the fresh scat of the wombat on a nearby rock. We see the wind direction and the fresh tracks that tell us about the animal's behaviour and condition.

We see no sign of recent snake activity. We see a thousand things and know that the wombat is alive and inside the log. We see this because we are not observing the log, but we are an integral part of the dynamic system of that Country, which is observing itself. So we share in the exchange of energy and information in that system and are therefore not intervening in the system with the act of outsider observation/ intervention.

Intervention from outside of a system is therefore a clear violation of the Law of the Land, particularly if that intervention is based on contaminated data and wrong story tainted by observer effects. There are many basic aspects of the Law of the Land that can be found through studying the laws of physics. Violations of First Law occur when these basic laws are ignored, laws that can be expressed in simple ways that you don't need to be a scientist or Elder to understand. You can't take more than what there is. It is easier to break stuff than make stuff. Energy, information and resources are distributed evenly in a sustainable system.

There must be free movement and exchange of everything in a sustainable system. Respect yourself and the Land by recognising that you are a part of it. You cannot intervene unilaterally in the Land and its communities from the outside.

While humans uphold this Law, the Land itself will administer it when we fail to meet our obligations as a custodial species. It can take five hundred to a thousand years for the Law of the Land to terminate a community that continues to break the Law, as can be seen in the relatively recent written histories of the rise and fall of civilisations. Every civilisation based on extraction, infinite growth and expansion is terminated in this way, and it is a punishment that is inescapable. Nobody can escape the laws of physics, so it is a good idea to adhere to First Law wherever possible, no matter what your culture of origin.

3.7.6 Place for Second Lore

Perhaps a new Story is needed for this. Each landmark stands as an entity of lore that upholds the Law. The lore, the narratives of Lands and waters and skies, carry cautionary tales so that every stone and star and waterhole contains a reminder of how to behave on Country and in community, and how to organise governance and economic systems within the bounds of First Law. This lore also reminds us of the consequences of lawlessness. Without that lore, we have no access to Law and sustainable ways of living.

The Goose that Laid the Golden Egg is an important Northern Hemisphere story that should govern the way Europeans manage resources. However, it does not work because there is not a corresponding landscape or Songline to make the lore real. If there were a hill that was the body of that golden goose, with a waterway leading to its severed head a mile away, then a ridge that you might follow to find the boulder that is the last of the golden eggs, then this might be a bit of lore that could carry Law. It could be real, if there were a Story map and a place for it. There are new landforms, new built environments and abandoned open-cut mines that could stand as physical entities in new Story, new cautionary tales to communicate First Law for future generations. There are landfill sites, scars and eroded areas and crime scenes of genocide and biocide that need to be connected with living Story in order for healing to take place and Law to be re-embedded within every community living on this continent. We all need to become keepers of this lore.

3.7.7 Certainty

The First Law of First Peoples aligns in its most basic principles with the laws of physics and nature. This is the point of entry for beginners who are seeking to understand Indigenous jurisprudence. As a novice gains more experience and understanding through bringing these stories alongside each other and then being on Country as a living part of the sentient landscape, then they become ready to receive higher knowledge about First Law. It is appropriate that this entry-level story is being produced and shared by an Aboriginal person with the cultural status and knowledge of an adolescent.

I am a boy belonging to the Apalech Clan from Western Cape York, living within the Law of my own clan but also the greater continental common Law that exists in an ancient network of Songlines and ceremony sites all over Australia. I don't have very much knowledge, but still I live within the Law of the Land and carry enough Story to live my life without breaking First Law. I am able to engage with global knowledge and interact within the global economy while applying First Law in ways that enrich this experience for myself and all others I come into relation with in my work. The most important message to take from this story is that First Law is accessible for everybody and has the capacity to engage all people in the vital work of creating regenerative systems in every area of human endeavour. I know only one thing for certain. If we are unable to bring settlers back under the Law of the Land, then everything and everyone here will soon die.

3.8 Shola Diop

South Sea Islander Kastom

Biography

My experiences and understanding of First Law and more importantly, societal dualities is inextricably linked to my proud tri-cultural heritage. On my father's side I am of Nigerian descent, with heritage reaching the Yoruba tribe. On my mother's side, I am of proud Australian South Sea Islander descent with our heritage stretching to Tanna (Tanauta) Island, Vanuatu. For the purpose of this case study, I will draw on my experiences as an Australian South Sea Islander due to our resilience and ingenuity in societal plurality as a historically dispossessed people. I have chosen to tell my story through a comprehensive retelling of my family's history and its connection to the broader plight of Australian South Sea Islanders on this Country. I have then chosen to explore specific forms of kastom (custom) particularly the concept of 'Wantok' and assess its practical contemporary use in plurality across different mediums.

3.8.1 Family History

No Australian South Sea Islanders story can be told in isolation. Each one of us is invariably a collection of stories, each weaving a convoluted series of paths back to the islands our ancestors were taken from. The most well-known story of our family's origins on this Country is that of my great grandfather, Moses Topay Enares. Moses was 12 years old when he was kidnapped out of the water swimming with two other boys in the late 1800s. They were tricked into boarding a ship that took them away from their families and homelands of Tanauta Island (aka Tanna), Vanuatu, to join the hordes of people taken through Australia's dark Blackbirding slave trade.

Conversely, my great grandmother, named as Emily May Enares (nee Santo/ Sendy), lived most of her life in NSW and was the first generation born descendant of a female child servant stolen from the island of Ambae (formerly Aoba), aged approximately 14 years old. Emily was estranged from her father, believed to be Terry (Tarry) Santo, who came from a mission or reserve in Hervey Bay (Butchulla Country) Queensland. Emily was born on a plantation in Maryborough (Gubbi Gubbi Country) Queensland. She was raised by my great-great-grandmother, known as granny Toar, Sarah Booky (Bouky) Toar (Toa). She and Moses had 11 children, which included my grandmother Nellie Enares. My grandmother's cultural heritage and family name 'Santo' 'Toar' 'Toa' can be traced to the Cape York region of Aboriginal Australia and Melanesian regions of Townsville and the Torres Strait Islands (Bamaga), Papua New Guinea, Vanuatu and the Solomon Islands.

The region which includes Cape York area is historically known as black Oceania. She also had part of an unidentified heritage from Polynesia. From an Australian South Sea Islander cultural perspective, I equate these mixed genealogies with being part of the vast Melanesian region of Australia where many First Nations/South Sea Islander/Australian South Sea Islander histories and living memories originate.

3.8.2 Australian South Sea Islander History: Blackbirding and Forced Migration

The people today known as Australian South Sea Islanders are a distinct cultural group whose roots on this Country can be traced back to a dark time in Australia's colonial history. Blackbirding formally known as the 'Indentured Labour Trade' was a practice endorsed and administered by the Commonwealth Government between 1863 and 1904. The trade saw approximately 62,475 Pacific Islanders enter Australia (predominantly Queensland) under contracts of indentured servitude, many of whom were forcibly removed or coerced from their homelands. Most were adolescent and young adult males; only about 5% were women.

The culture of today's Australian South Sea Islander community is shaped by their treatment during the indentured labour period and the harsh years early in the twentieth century. Their sense of their united history begins in 1863 with the first labour recruits. Australian South Sea Islanders refer to themselves as the descendants of slaves, and it is clear that the community harbours a deep sense of injustice.

In 1901 the new Commonwealth Government passed the *Pacific Island Labourers Act*, part of a package of legislation to achieve a White Australia. The aim was to remove Pacific Islanders from Australia through gradual attrition (those on new three-year contracts entered into up until the end of 1903) and forced deportation. Only 839 'ticket-holders' (pre-1879 arrivals) were exempt. This racist legislation was in line with the sentiments of the majority of the parliamentarians and the Australian people. To compensate the sugar industry the Australian government introduced an embargo on all 'foreign sugar' and a bonus for sugar produced using only white labour. This transition was well in place by 1906 and by 1911 94% of the labour in the sugar industry was provided by Europeans.

Forced deportation began in late 1906 and continued until mid-1908. Families were ripped apart and property was forfeited. On return to the islands many faced severe problems readjusting to their old lives and some were killed. The official number allowed to remain was 1,654, but later estimates suggest that around 2,500 remained. The result was a cruel, racially-based mass deportation unique in Australian history and a matter of shame for the Australian government and people.

In 1992 the Australian Human Rights and Equal Opportunity Commission published a Book which called for recognition of the ASSI community as a distinct ethnic group within Australia. This was followed by Commonwealth recognition in 1994. In 1995 NSW Premier Bob Carr advised ministers to include ASSI's in all programs and services. This memorandum has been overlooked to date. In 2000 Premier Peter Beattie recognised ASSI in Queensland. Despite these official gestures there was little sustained government assistance to the ASSI community.

An important agenda for Australian South Sea Islander people living in Australia today, second and third generation Australians of South Sea Islander heritage, is to reconnect with their families in the islands, undo the radical rupture of families that occurred during the 60–70 years of slavery and seek to re-establish some genealogical continuity. There are also many families in the islands seeking connection with their lost families in Australia.

3.8.3 *Kinship (Aboriginal and Torres Strait Islander Connections)*

Today there are about 100 Australian South Sea Islander families, the majority of which have kin connections, through blood or marriage, with the Aboriginal community.

The Australian South Sea Islander connection to the Torres Strait is somewhat more profound given hundreds of South Sea Islanders were taken to the Torres Strait from 1860 until about 1880, to work in the pearl and bêche-de-mer industries. Most of these people intermarried into the local Torres Strait Islander families. It is surmised that around 50–60% of Torres Strait Islanders would have some ASSI ancestry.

3.8.4 *Kastom (Customary Law from a Pacific Perspective)*

As a largely dispossessed people with an amalgamation of cultural and linguistic roots, Australian South Sea Islanders struggle with the assertion of any single form of First Law. As such, an effective through-line for Australian South Sea Islanders emerges in the customary concepts that run consistently across the various Melanesian cultures that we originate from. The term 'kastom' (denoting customary practice) has been used at various times in relation to Australian South Sea Islander relations with their families and nations in the Pacific. Kastom is a Pijin term that can refer to shared traditions, but also to ideas and institutions perceived to be grounded in Indigenous concepts and principles.

Thus 'kastom' is not, as is often supposed, synonymous with the English 'custom', which is typically conceived as Melanesian ways from before Europeans' arrival in the islands. Particularly in its political uses, kastom is often closely tied to Indigenous means of dispute resolution, or 'kastom loa', set in opposition to state or 'government law'. The word has developed different meanings in different Melanesian countries and cultures. Kastom is a fluid concept that is used selectively and creatively and is for many ni-Vanuatu and Solomon Islanders a key mechanism for adapting to and channelling modernisation and change. While kastom is most often presented as authentic and traditional, it underpins local circumstances, rights and interpretations and shifts over time. Kastom began to coalesce in the nineteenth and early twentieth centuries, but it is not the same as customs 'practiced for generations'.

Throughout the Pacific, governance structures vary enormously, and many nations have incorporated aspects of customary governance. These modern structures include features of governments world-wide and aspects of the original forms of authority. For example, the original systems in Melanesia (New Guinea, Solomon Islands, Vanuatu and New Caledonia, with Fiji on the cusp with Polynesia) owe most to the Bigmen system where successful entrepreneurs were influential secular leaders. Customary governance is hereditary in some areas, particularly in Polynesia and

Micronesia. For instance, Tonga has had a monarchy since 1857 when high chieftainships were combined into one position. Independence was restored in 1970 and a Privy Council began, comprised of the King, the Cabinet and the Governors of Vava'u and Haapai. The Parliament comprised nine nobles elected by the 33 nobles, along with nine elected representatives of the public, and the King's appointees who included the Prime Minister and Cabinet. Recently there has been a move toward a more democratic Parliament but effective power rests with the King and his nobility.

Similarly, Samoa was a chiefly society and in 1962 at independence the National Parliament consisted of 47 elected members, 45 of whom must be chiefs. Until 1990 only chiefs could vote for these members, but thereafter although only chiefs can stand, any adult may vote. In Fiji the chiefly system remains at the heart of the political and socioeconomic system. Fiji began with an elected monarchy under Chief Cakabau. Even in British times (1874–1970), Fiji allowed special emphasis on chiefs, and after independence, created a hereditary council of chiefs alongside its lower house. The head of state is elected by the Great Council of Chiefs, after consultation with the Prime Minister.

The Pacific Island customary principles that invariably form parts of the Australian South Sea Islander genealogy show viable examples of the active plurality between kastom and Western law. However, while the concept of kastom is an undeniably central part to our spirit and identity, our modern history of forced removal and dispossession has seen a disconnection between the average Australian South Sea Islander and kastom. Despite the odds, a profound influence of kastom is still evident in the evolution of Australian South Sea Islander culture and our historic efforts to thrive against the odds.

3.8.5 Wantok (Contemporary Adaptations of Kastom)

Historically, culturally diverse languages such as Pijin English are a combination of English words with grammatical structures from the Pacific region and Indigenous Australia. Pijin English is also called Tok Pisin, Solomon's Pijin, and Bislama, which is the common language spoken throughout the Pacific, and more recently, taught as part of the Vanuatu curriculum. Bislama was developed during the 1860s to 1880s as an organic means of communication between Indigenous peoples of Australia and the Pacific, and as a means of communication with colonisers.

Creole is spoken mainly in the Torres Strait by descendants of the Blackbirding trade, with a small increase of Bislama and Solomons' Pijin on the mainland, as descendants have been relinking with our families and cultural practices in Australia and the Pacific. Australian South Sea Islander contemporary culture has adopted specific terminology from the nineteenth century that is used to identify the origins of our heritage. The term 'Wantok' is a kastom word that identifies kinship systems and means a common bond and knowingness across our Melanesian regions. It is used as a term of endearment in dialogue among members mainly of the Australian South Sea Islander community.

Traditionally, throughout many parts of Melanesia the term Wantok refers to:

> (…) a social system where people who are related to each other by a common language, ethnicity, district or by provincial boundaries (defined as 'wantoks') will jointly participate in sociopolitical, economic, traditional and cultural activities in Papua New Guinea society. It is a system where people depend on, care for, and help each other in many aspects of society. While traditionally family and clan members were obligated to provide support for each other, the wantok system today performs a set of broader roles. It acts, for example, as a form of social security, whereby families look after their sick or elderly family members.[40]

From an Australian South Sea Islander perspective, the term Wantok has been adapted in many ways in our continued fight for social justice, community development and community cohesion. My own experience of the adaptation of Wantok has been through its practical use in social rights advocacy. In 2009, we began our work for the advocacy of Australian South Sea Islander social justice and inclusion with the incorporation of the NGO Australian South Sea Islanders, Port Jackson (ASSI.PJ), lead by Chairwoman (Waskam) Emelda Davis.

The mandate for ASSI.PJ was to usher in an era of truth-telling and reckoning for the broader Australian society to recognise the atrocities of Blackbirding and its role in building the Australian narrative. ASSI.PJ also set out to highlight the tremendous contributions of Australian South Sea Islanders as a distinct cultural group and work to foster community development and cohesion between Australian South Sea Islanders across the Country. As a part of this feat, in 2012 we set out to formalise the formation of an Australian South Sea Islander National body, one that would present a unified voice for the continued advocacy for the social inclusion and development of our people.

While our approach to this national body formation sought to adopt a regimented democratic process that would include a wide array of Australian South Sea Islander voices, it was important to implement this process through the lens of a cultural framework that spoke to the many Melanesian bloodlines that connected our communities. Thus, between 2012 and 2015, ASSI.PJ hosted a series of seven 'Wantok' national workshops held at various sites across the Country. The purpose of the workshops was to create a culturally appropriate and safe platform through which Australian South Sea Islanders could congregate and be represented in the planning, election and formation of a national body.

The Wantok series saw almost 1200 Australian South Sea Islanders representing from over 20 regions of NSW and Queensland. It also included Vanuatu government and Chiefs from our respective island regions as well as other international community members and academics. The series signified the largest democratic process seen by the ASSI community to date. This resulted in the formation of the National Australian South Sea Islander Association Constitution and the nomination of delegates.

---

[40] Tok Pisin English Dictionary. (2015). Available at: https://www.tokpisin.info/wantok-system-pngs-safety-net/.

Contemporary applications of the concept of Wantok can also been seen in certain parts of the Pacific to signal a unified resistance against climate change largely driven by Western fossil fuel dependency as well as water and Land degradation.

The 2019 film *Wantoks: Dance of Resilience in Melanesia*[41] produced and directed by Lara Lee, profiles artists and activists who are fighting for self-determination while trying to defend their homes against the rising sea. The film premiered in Helsinki, Finland, in May 2019, and is now screening around the globe. In all Melanesian countries, residents face the common challenge of climate change, as rising sea levels threaten to swallow both Land and tradition. Within the film, captivating performers are using their talents to celebrate local culture and draw international attention to their islands' plight, with the hope of spurring international solidarity and prompting collective action against the perils of global warming.

Other examples can be seen where the practical application of Wantok concepts can be used in the advocacy and program design of climate and Land rights within a Western context. The UK-based Wantok Support Charity originated by the former Papua New Guinea High Commissioner to the United Kingdom, specialises in improving the lives of the citizens of Papua New Guinea (PNG), focusing on environmental, healthcare and education issues.

Alternatively, the Wantok Environment Centre (WTEC) is a national environmental non-government incorporation in Vanuatu that operates as a charitable association. Its mission is the care and protection of Vanuatu's natural environment, recognising its importance for all forms of life, for present and future generations and in the sustainable development of the Country. WTEC's primary concern is representing the interests of rural communities and families directly involved in the conservation and/or sustainable management of Vanuatu's natural environment and resource.

Examination of these contemporary applications of the concept of Wantok with my own experience reveals a powerful brand of advocacy that is rooted in a custom of kinship and reciprocity. While it can be conceded that these examples superficially supplant the concept of Wantok to select social and environmental issues, it is worth noting that its use by South Sea and Australian South Sea Islanders alike signifies an honoring of kastom and First Law. It also displays an ingenuity of Wantok's application to a Western context in the twenty-first century. Also, as noted the Wantok system has widespread influence in many Melanesian countries and provides a tangible example of active forms of legal plurality. Therefore Wantok, as well as other forms of societal and linguistic kastom holds a great deal of potential in examining First Law as an effective interface with Australian South Sea Islanders and their Aboriginal, Torres Strait Islander and South Pacific Islander bloodlines.

[41] Lee (2019).

3.9 Donna Bagnall

Healthy Law, Healthy Country

Note Please refer to 4.2, which contains detailed findings by Donna Bagnall of legal cases in Australia that are pertinent in the context of this paper.

Biography

My lived experience, knowledge and wisdom that I bring to this book derives from my ancestry, my academic background, the people I have grown up with, and the friends and colleagues I have collaborated with and shared knowledge and wisdom with throughout my lifetime.

My ancestry includes both 'First Nations' and 'First Fleet'—my Great-Great Grandfather (my mother's mother's grandfather) was an Aboriginal man from Manning River (Birpai Country); and my five times Great-grandfather on my mother's father's side was a convict from Cornwall, a county in south-west England, who was sentenced to transportation to Australia, sailing on the Scarborough in 1788 with the First Fleet. I also have ancestors from Scotland, Ireland and Sweden on my father's side. My Swedish two times Great-grandfather on my father's side was born in Stockholm and was a ship's captain who sailed to Australia early last century. I therefore inherently bring with me and represent a rich blend of cultural histories, genealogy, values, experiences and wisdoms that have influenced my perspectives—both my conscious and subconscious, and my physical and spiritual being- notably a close ancestral connection to water.

From my academic studies in Western law, commerce and sustainability, my professional work as a tax policy adviser, and my collaborative research[42] since 2015 with Professor Anne Poelina, Nyikina Warrwa woman and Traditional Custodian, to protect the Martuwarra (Fitzroy River) in the Kimberley, Western Australia, I have acquired a broad range of knowledge which equips me to view the world from many different perspectives, i.e. I am a 'polymath'.

---

[42] RiverOfLife et al. (2020c).

I have intentionally developed skills and knowledge across many disciplines: Law; Policy; Tax/Economics; Accounting/Reporting; R&D/Innovation/Technology; Sustainability/Climate change/Science; Indigenous Culture, First Law and Regional governance; Arts/Humanities/Linguistics. Viewing issues at the intersection of multiple or all of these subject matters assists me with problem-solving, and in developing strategies and new approaches which may not yet have been considered. Through this transdisciplinary lens, I understand the connections and 'join the dots' to see the bigger picture and how things interrelate.

To my mind, the single most significant piece of Western knowledge I have acquired from my life-long academic learnings,[43] culminating in my Master of Sustainability and Climate Policy, is the wisdom of sustainability principles. Yet, these are the principles that Australia's Indigenous peoples have understood from the beginning of time, passed down by the ancestors through First Law–namely, that everything is connected and cyclical, and that our world is made up of complex, dynamic 'systems within systems', and interdependent relationships, in which people are a part of, not separate from, the natural world.

To stay healthy and balanced, each sub-system, each relationship and each being must receive what it needs to survive and thrive, and it must reciprocate to ensure the other sub-systems, relationships and beings also receive what they need. Without this, our natural systems and social processes are unsustainable and will not provide any lasting wellbeing or prosperity.

First Law embodies and lives these principles through its laws, customs, culture and language—laws of relationships, respect, reciprocity, care and interdependency with nature.[44]

The Songlines, Jukurrpa (Dreamings) and totems are "a common property institution for long-term ecological management".[45] They also serve to convey the laws, and in this sense are akin to the statutes.[46]

Indeed, 'Jukurrpa', a Warlpiri word, has been defined in this way:

> The term Jukurrpa may be applied to **individual ancestral beings, or to any manifestation of their power and nature**, i.e. knowledge of their travels and activities, rituals, designs, songs, places, ceremonies. This **provides the model for human and non-human activity, social behaviour, natural development**. Jukurrpa is not conceived as being located in an historical past but **as an eternal process which involves the maintenance of these lifeforces**, symbolized as men and as other natural species.[47]

---

[43] The second most significant is my knowledge and understanding of the law, in addition to First Law, because of its power to achieve justice, equity, substantive equality and transformative change to care for our Earth, our only home.

[44] Redvers et al. (2020b).

[45] Bird Rose (2013).

[46] Dr Anne Poelina, Personal Communication, 10 June 2021.

[47] Goddard and Wierzbicka (2015), p. 44, citing Laughren et al. (2006).

3.9.1 *First Law (Indigenous Customary Law or Traditional Law)*

Songlines, Jukurrpa and totem systems are the application of First Law 'through multilayered stories that impart values and ethics; thus they represent a comprehensive ethical framework that defines the codes of conduct necessary for maintaining a peaceful, thriving, and co-operative society grounded in love and reciprocity'.[48] Together, they are a system of laws, values and principles for a sustainable Mother Earth, fused with spirituality and sourced in ethics of care and responsibility.[49]

Implicit in these understandings are also the obligations of guardianship, intergenerational responsibility and precautionary stewardship to maintain the balance and harmony of these natural systems and relationships.[50] First Law is based on ancient inherited science, philosophies and laws, so this means that Indigenous Nations have a duty of care to apply this wisdom for the benefit of their First People, all Australians and world citizens.[51]

The wisdom of First Law comes from the '*Bookarrarra*'—the beginning of time fused with the present and the future in the same moment.[52] As Marlikka Perdrisat, Nyikina Warrwa Wangkumara Barkindji woman has elucidated, this means that "we have to use the past, in the present moment, to protect the future".[53] In a similar vein, newly appointed Governor-General of New Zealand, Dame Cindy Kiro, a Māori woman with British ancestry—who embodies a unique marriage of customary law and Western law—neatly encapsulated the meaning of 'wisdom' in her recent acceptance speech, when she remarked:

> I'm a strong believer in the importance of knowledge, but more importantly of wisdom. Wisdom is the distilled knowledge born of the experience of ethical behaviour.[54]

The distilled knowledge born of the experience of ethical behaviour is something that has been sorely missing from Australia's legal system over the past two centuries and three decades. Instead, the Western law has been willfully used to inequitably mistreat and exclude our Indigenous peoples from their rightful place of ethically caring for their traditional Lands and waters.

Australia has the rare privilege of being home to the wisdom of First Law held by our First Peoples—the Aboriginal and Torres Strait Islander Peoples. Australia should have the wisdom and the strategic vision to embrace First Law and fully incorporate it into Australian law, as we have the opportunity for it to evolve into one of the most 'fit for purpose' legal systems on planet Earth.

---

48 Redvers et al., op. cit.

49 RiverOfLife et al., op. cit.

50 RiverOfLife et al., op. cit.

51 Perdrisat (2021).

52 Excellence Reporter (2018).

53 Perdrisat, Jakamarra, & Poelina, op. cit.

54 Women's Agenda (2021).

3.9.2 How Do We Achieve the Mission of 'Healthy Law, Healthy Country'?

Fulfilling the mission statement of 'Healthy Law, Healthy Country' in Australia will be dependent upon the legal profession, our legal institutions and our law and policymakers adopting a truly plural Australian legal system.

Based on my research and knowledge of the system of First Law, and my lived experience as a lawyer in the Australian Western legal system, I consider that the overarching objective of implementing legal pluralism in Australia broadly involves **three main goals**: (i) remedy the Australian Western law, as it is sick and in decay; (ii) duly recognise, protect and enforce First Law in the Australian legal system and (iii) embed principles consistent with First Law within the Australian policy making framework.

While major medium-long-term goals and steps, such as Constitutional reform, Referendum on 'Voice, Treaty, Truth' and an Australian Republic, are not the focus of this story, the three goals considered in this paper would support and promote those broader goals.[55]

We now explore this in greater detail.

References

Allam, L. (2021). A journey down WA's Mighty Martuwarra, Raging River and Sacred Ancestor. [Podcast]. Available at: https://www.theguardian.com/australia-news/audio/2021/dec/31/a-journey-down-was-mighty-martuwarra-raging-river-and-sacred-ancestor.

Australian Conservation Foundation. (2021). *Forging the forever industries: How ancient wisdom can guide the transition to new economies*. Available at: https://acf.exposure.co/forging-the-forever-industries

Bird Rose, D. (2013). Common property regimes in aboriginal Australia: Totemism Revisited. In P. Larmour (Ed.), *The governance of common property in the Pacific Region* (pp. 127–143). ANU Press. Available at: http://press-files.anu.edu.au/downloads/press/p229161/pdf/ch092.pdf

Black, C. F. (2011). *The land is the source of the law: A dialogic encounter with indigenous jurisprudence.* Routledge Cavendish.

Descartes, R. (1999). *Discourse on Method and Meditations on First Philosophy.* Translated by Donald A. Cress. Hackett Publishing, p. 65

Excellence Reporter. (2018). *Dr Anne Poelina: The meaning of life and the law of the land*. Available at: https://excellencebooker.com/2018/03/08/dr-anne-poelina-the-meaning-of-life-and-the-law-of-the-land/

Goddard, C., & Wierzbicka, A. (2015). *What does Jukurrpa ('Dreamtime', 'the Dreaming') mean?* Australian National University.

Graham, M. (2009a). Indigenous community centred planning (ICCP) strategy: Scoping paper (unpublished).

Graham, M. (2009b). Understanding human agency in terms of place: A proposed Aboriginal research methodology. *PAN: Philosophy Activism Nature*, *6*, 71–78.

[55] Uluru Statement from the Heart (2017). *Voice, Treaty, Truth.* Available at: https://ulurustatement.org/.

Graham, M. (2014). Aboriginal notions of relationality and positionalism: A reply to weber. *Global Discourse, 4*(1), 17–22. https://doi.org/10.1080/23269995.2014.895931

Laughren et al. (2006). *Warlpiri-English Encyclopaedic Dictionary*.

Lee, L. (2019). *Wantoks: Dance of Resilience in Melanesia.* [Online Film]. Cultures of Resistance Films. Available at: https://culturesofresistancefilms.com/wantoks/

Lim, M. (2017). RiverOfLife, Martuwarra Fitzroy River Council, Lim, & McDuffie

Martuwarra Fitzroy River Council. (2016). *Fitzroy River Declaration.* Available at: http://majala.com.au/news/protecting-the-fitzroy-river-catchment

Maybury-Lewis, D. (Director). (1992). Millenium: Tribal wisdom and the modern world [Television Series]. Canada: Biniman Productions Ltd; Adrian Malone Productions Ltd; KCET; BBC TV; The Global Television Network; Rogers Telefund; Telefilm Canada.

Perdrisat, M. (2021). AIATSIS Summit Keynote speech. Available at: https://aiatsis.gov.au/presentation/summit-keynote-marlikka-perdrisat

Perdrisat, M., Jakamarra, H., & Poelina, A. (2021). Bookarrarra. [Online Video]. Available at: https://vimeo.com/451420394.

Poelina, A., & McDuffie, M. (2019a). *Balkinjirr Poem* [Online Video]. Madjulla Inc & Ngikalikarra Media. Available at: https://vimeo.com/376460849

Poelina, A., & McDuffie, M. (2019b). *Singing Yoongoorrookoo* [Online Video]. Madjulla Inc; Harry's Collar; Ngikalikarra Media. Available at: https://vimeo.com/376460849

Poelina, A., Marshall, L., Warbie, J., & McDuffie, M. (2015). *Three sisters, women of high degree.* [Film]. Available at: https://ictv.com.au/video/item/6499

Poelina, A., Perdrisat, I., & McDuffie, M. (2016). Mardoowarra, River of Life. [Online Video]. Madjulla Inc. Available at: https://vimeo.com/187590078/7afbbc772d

Poelina, A., Taylor, K. S., & Perdrisat, I. (2019). Martuwarra Fitzroy River Council: An Indigenous cultural approach to collaborative water governance. *Australasian Journal of Environmental Management*, *26*(3), 236–254. Available at: https://doi.org/10.1080/14486563.2019.1651226

Poelina, A. (2020). A coalition of hope! a regional governance approach to indigenous australian cultural wellbeing. In A. Campbell, M. Duffy, & B. Edmondson (Eds.). *Located research: Regional places, transitions and challenges* (pp. 153–180). Springer Singapore. Available at: https://doi.org/10.1007/978-981-32-9694-7_10

Poelina, A., Wooltorton, S., Harben, S., Collard, L., Horwitz, P., & Palmer, D. (2020a). Feeling and Hearing Country. *PAN: Philosophy, Activism, Nature, 5*, 6–15. Available at: https://bridges.monash.edu/articles/journal_contribution/Feeling_and_Hearing_Country/13461098/1

Poelina, A., Bruecker, M., & McDuffie, M. (2020b). For the greater good: Questioning the social licence of extractive-led development in Western Australia's Martuwarra Fitzroy River Region. *The Extractive Industries and Society*, *8*(3), 19. Available at: https://doi.org/10.1016/j.exis.2020.10.010

Redvers, N., Poelina, A., Schultz, C., Kobei, D.M., Githaiga, C., Perdrisat, M., Prince, D., & Blondin, B. (2020a). Indigenous natural and first law in planetary health. *Challenges, 11*(23). Available at: https://doi.org/10.3390/challe11020029

Redvers, N., Poelina, A., Schultz, C., Kobei, D., Githaiga, C., Perdrisat, M., Prince, D., & Blondin, B. (2020b). Indigenous natural or first law in planetary health. *Challenges*, *11*(2), 29. Available at: https://doi.org/10.3390/challe11020029

RiverOfLife, M., Martuwarra Fitzroy River Council, Lim, M., & McDuffie, M. (2017). An Interview with Michelle Lim. [Online Video]. Available at: https://vimeo.com/433343821/0023e84b48

RiverOfLife, M., Brown, J., Martuwarra Fitzroy River Council, & King, S. (2020a). Joe Brown: Martuwarra. Available at: https://vimeo.com/546836156/8b3eb7f6e7

RiverOfLife, M., McDuffie, M., & Poelina, A., (2020b). *Martuwarra country: A historical perspective (1838-present).* Martuwarra Fitzroy River Council; Nulungu Research Institute, The University of Notre Dame Australia. https://doi.org/10.32613/nrp/2020.5

RiverOfLife, M., Poelina, A., Bagnall, D., & Lim, M. (2020c). Recognising the Martuwarra's first law right to life as a living ancestral being. *Transnational Environmental Law, 9*(3), 541–568. Available at: https://doi.org/10.1017/S2047102520000163

RiverOfLife, M., Poelina, A., Alexandra, J., Samnakay, N. (2020d). A Conservation and Management Plan for the National Heritage listed Fitzroy River Catchment Estate (No. 1). Martuwarra Fitzroy River Council, Nulungu Research Institute, The University of Notre Dame Australia. Available at: https://doi.org/10.32613/nrp/2020.4

RiverOfLife, M., Taylor, K. S., & Poelina, A. (2021a). Living waters, law first: Nyikina and Mangala water governance in the Kimberley, Western Australia. *Australasian Journal of Water Resources, 25*(1). Available at: https://doi.org/10.1080/13241583.2021.1880538

RiverOfLife, M., Poelina, A., & McDuffie, M. (2021b). Martuwarra, River of Life. [Online Video]. Available at: https://vimeo.com/533047074/87705efc9e

Tobin, B. (2014). Indigenous peoples, customary law and human rights-why living law matters. Routledge.

Watson, I. (2015). Aboriginal peoples, colonialism and international law: raw law. Routledge.

Women's Agenda. (2021). Dame Cindy Kiro named next Governor-General of NZ becoming first Maori woman to take the role. Available at: https://womensagenda.com.au/leadership/cindy-kiro-named-next-governor-general-of-nz-becoming-first-maori-woman-to-take-the-role/

Yunkaporta, T. (2019). *Sand talk: How indigenous thinking can save the world*. The Text Publishing Company.

Chapter 4
How We Can Change the Current Legal System

In this section, we outline a number of different ways that Western law could be changed in Australia. In theory, none of these approaches are mutually exclusive.

In summary, these approaches are:

- Integrate Indigenous knowledge and 'First Laws' into Western law;
- Shift Western law towards Earth Laws (Earth jurisprudence and 'ecological law'), which can lay stronger foundations within Western law to support First Laws;
- Recognise Indigenous Sovereignty and Privilege First Laws;
- Advocate for and develop the jurisprudence of legal pluralism in Australia.

4.1 Summary of Different Approaches

4.1.1 Integrate First Laws into, or with Western Laws

When considering broad approaches to changing the current Western legal system in Australia, it is first worth reflecting on the dominant approach in many progressive modern legal systems (international law and the domestic law of colonial nations), which sees the integration of Indigenous law and cultural practices 'into' Western law as a way forward.

While this has the benefit of strengthening Western laws' capacity to protect and reflect Indigenous peoples' values, it also continues a colonial mindset of keeping Western law as the dominant system, and merely 'allowing' Indigenous law into small elements of the overarching legal system. But there are different approaches to integrating different legal systems, Indigenous and non-Indigenous, and different perspectives on what such integration means or implies. For the present project we point to some critical questions to consider, which include: matters of differential power and authority; modalities of integration, i.e. how the different systems work together; and the relative roles and responsibilities of key participants in integrating

A. Poelina et al., *Declaration of Peace for Indigenous Australians and Nature*,
https://doi.org/10.1007/978-981-99-9327-7_4

systems. Another central element in examining the integration of legal systems is the complex relationship between law and state.

International Law—Biocultural Laws, Shifts to Integration

Here we examine one aspect of integrating different types of legal systems, in the context of international environment and biodiversity conservation. Within this broad legal arena, the emergence of biocultural rights, as a distinct order of rights that has the capacity to embrace both Indigenous and environmental rights, appears to offer an opportunity for Western nation states to bring Indigenous customary laws and Western legal regimes together (albeit still within the Western international legal system). Biocultural rights also offer potential for nation states to build what might be more inclusive ways of recognising and protecting Indigenous legal and cultural systems in plural formations. The 1992 United Nations *Convention on Biological Diversity*, at articles 8(j) and 10(c), provides for the protection of Indigenous knowledge and customary laws relevant to access and fair and equitable sharing of the benefits of the use of biological resources. The 2010 *Nagoya Protocol on Access to Genetic Resources and the Fair and Equitable Sharing of Benefits Arising from their Utilization to the Convention on Biological Diversity* take this further.

Bavikatte and Bennett argue that 'biocultural rights' can offer 'community-led' solutions to the 'current ecological crisis'.[1] They describe these rights as a "community's long-established right, in accordance with its customary laws, to steward its Lands, waters and resources".[2] These biocultural rights are the "collective rights of communities to carry out traditional stewardship roles vis-a-vis Nature, as conceived of by Indigenous ontologies".[3] The term biocultural rights, these authors explain, "has been used widely by communities, academics and civil society to indicate a way of life that has developed out of a holistic relationship between Nature and culture. Hence, biocultural rights affirm the bond between Indigenous, tribal and other communities with their Land, together with the floral, faunal and other resources in and on the Land". This relationship, as these authors note, is often denoted as a form of 'stewardship'.[4]

Bavikatte and Bennett chart the emergence of biocultural rights, claiming these derive in part, from the failure of 'top-down' development scenarios in protecting the environment.[5] These 'third generation' collective rights[6] include Indigenous peoples' and minority rights. These authors explain the links between Indigenous, environmental and biocultural rights:

> Biocultural rights emerged contemporaneously with the appearance of environmental and indigenous rights, but almost unnoticed. These rights differ from the general category of

[1] Bavikatte and Bennett (2015), at p. 27, p. 8.

[2] Ibid., p. 7.

[3] Ibid.

[4] Ibid., p. 8.

[5] Ibid., p. 9.

[6] Ibid., pp. 10–11.

> indigenous rights because they presuppose an explicit link to the conservation and the sustainable use of biological diversity, and because the group need not necessarily be indigenous. The word 'biocultural' is a catchall term that connects communities, Land and its resources, its tenure systems and its ecosystems.[7]
>
> Biocultural rights therefore denote all the rights required to secure community stewardship over their Lands and waters. This role reflects a way of life, whereby a community's identity, its culture, spirituality and system of governance are inseparable from its Lands and waters. Biocultural rights do not denote exercise of ownership in the Western legal sense but rather a duty of care and protection.[8]

The concept of biocultural rights is also supportive of recognition of customary laws.[9] Bavikatte and Bennett argue that "a new legal landscape has emerged in which biocultural rights are being developed as a people-led alternative to state-led solutions to the environmental crisis".[10] The concept of biocultural rights is also discussed by others.[11] Bavikatte and Robinson place the concept of biocultural rights in the context of the *Nagoya Protocol for Access and Benefit-Sharing.* They assert that this Protocol "could certainly be seen as an expansion of 'cosmopolitan legality' which, we argue, has led/is leading to what could best be called new forms of 'biocultural jurisprudence'".[12] They also claim that, through this international instrument "the door in international law to legal pluralism and self-determination of Indigenous peoples and local communities was now ajar". These authors suggest that "In years to come, this achievement could see increased community rights and control over natural resources where they are the appropriate 'owners' or resource holders".[13] Chen and Gilmore also support the contention that biocultural rights frameworks offer opportunities for more holistic approaches to protection of Indigenous peoples' natural and cultural resources.[14] Similarly, Caillon et al. take the view that biocultural approaches to conservation "ground management in local knowledges, practices, and ontologies", and can address the divide between nature and culture through more inclusive and holistic management.[15]

Another writer on biocultural rights, Apgar, argues that these present opportunities for 'more inclusive environmental governance' for biodiversity management and conservation. Apgar explores biocultural approaches to environmental governance and conservation through analysing case studies of in-situ conservation of biocultural heritage.[16] Apgar's work is inspired by, among many scholars, the seminal writings of Elinor Ostrom (especially Ostrom 1990) whose work advocates for "self-governing

---

[7] Ibid., p. 10.

[8] Ibid., pp. 20–21.

[9] Ibid., p. 21.

[10] Ibid., p. 24.

[11] See, e.g., Bavikatte and Robinson (2011), Apgar (2017), Sajeva (2015), Chen and Gilmore (2015).

[12] Bavikatte and Robinson, op. cit., p. 40.

[13] Ibid., p. 46.

[14] Chen & Gilmore, op. cit.

[15] Caillon et al. (2017).

[16] Apgar, M. J., op. cit., p. 3.

approaches to collectively owned resources based on local institutions and practices that use place-specific knowledge embodied in communities".[17]

Apgar discusses the development of biocultural approaches that arose from the concept of biocultural diversity, tracing its growth through key work such as that by Darrell Posey, and Luisa Maffi among many. She writes:

> Biocultural approaches to conservation, governance and development all stem from the concept of biocultural diversity. The concept was built through the recognition of an inextricable link between traditional knowledge, the cultural and linguistic systems that knowledge is embedded in, and conservation of biodiversity (e.g. Posey, 2002). Biocultural diversity was first used as a metric to document, compare and analyse the links between linguistic, cultural and biological diversity.[18]

Apgar argues that biocultural environmental governance is situated within "broader interactional approaches that recognise a role for local spaces and knowledge".[19] Another proponent of biocultural rights is Sajeva who describes these as "all the rights of Indigenous peoples and local communities required to secure their stewardship role over their Lands and waters".[20] She argues that:

> Biocultural rights build on two foundations: the self-determination and cultural diversity of indigenous peoples and local communities, and the conservation of the environment. This article suggests that the second foundation is what makes biocultural rights potentially more appealing than other human rights but that it is also the reason for their sui generis potential.[21]

4.1.2 Shift Western Law Towards Earth Laws, Earth Jurisprudence and First Laws

In this book we use the term 'Earth Laws' to encapsulate the rapidly evolving field of Earth-centred or eco-centric legal theory and practice that includes: the philosophy of Earth jurisprudence, the legal issues and approaches included within the emerging field of 'ecological law',[22] the developing law of ecocide and rights-based legal approaches including Rights of Nature and 'legal personhood for nature'. These concepts and legal approaches are emerging within countries and jurisdictions around the world, as peoples in many different cultures and countries work to 'push back' and change the human-centred, extractivist Western legal systems that have supported environmental destruction. Many First Nations People—including several authors of this book—use the term 'Earth Laws', to refer to First Laws and emerging eco-centric laws within Western legal systems. In this book then, we use 'Earth Laws' as

[17] Ibid., p. 9. For the writings of Elinor Ostrom, see especially her *Governing the Commons: The Evolution of Institutions for Collective Action.* Cambridge University Press, 1990.

[18] Apgar, op. cit., p. 11. See also Maffi (2005), Posey (2002).

[19] Apgar, op. cit., p. 19.

[20] Sajeva (2015), p. 30.

[21] Ibid.

[22] For example, please see Anker et al. (2021).

a term that refers to a new legal paradigm that challenges the anthropocentrism and extractivism of Western law, and connects Western law with Indigenous First Laws. In this section we briefly review some of its key concepts from the perspective of Australian and Aboriginal law.

The philosophy of Earth jurisprudence can be a useful framework for connecting and understanding these diverse 'Earth Laws'. Earth jurisprudence is a term coined by deep ecologist and 'geologian' Thomas Berry. It is a theory that has emerged from within Western industrial society, to 'talk back' to and challenge, the devastating environmental and cultural impacts of Western industrial society.

In Australia, key concepts within Earth jurisprudence resonate very powerfully with people from the Western cultural tradition, as it helps people from this culture understand, 'unpack' and critique the deeply flawed basis of Western industrial society's approach to objectifying, commodifying and using up the living world.[23]

In his book *The Great Work: Our Way Into the Future,* Thomas Berry suggests that industrial society's laws, religious traditions, educational institutions and economic systems need to reflect and protect the bio-physical realities of the Earth Community. Earth jurisprudence advocates for a legal system with a number of critical elements; we briefly examine four of the foundational concepts below.

First, Earth jurisprudence acknowledges that the Universe is the *primary lawgiver*. In contrast to the current Western legal system that sees human laws as the highest authority for human society (and implicitly, for all other life forms and ecological systems), Earth jurisprudence sees the laws of the Universe, the 'Great Jurisprudence' or 'Great Law' as providing the fundamental parameters of the Earth Community, including human societies.[24] The concept of 'the Great Law' is seen as problematic even by many Western scholars. It is argued that it's very difficult to clarify what the Great Law is, or to specify how people can live within those laws.[25] Nonetheless, the idea that nature or the Universe is the primary lawgiver sees Earth jurisprudence as explicitly advocating for an idea of human societies living within the rules or limits of the natural world. In other words, it places human relationships with the non-human world as primary.

This concept, of a Great Law being the primary law, and human laws needing to fit within the Great Law, is in some ways, comparable to First Laws—the foundational idea that the Land is the source of the law. However, as First Nations peoples have lived by these First Laws since time immemorial, and these laws are connected to *specific regions and places* around Australia, it is difficult to compare them to the more 'general' rules articulated by Earth jurisprudence. Nonetheless, the idea of the Great Law is an important one to re-introduce to Western culture, as it begins the process of bringing Western people back to a sacred appreciation and respect for Mother Earth and can assist in the process of transforming the Western legal system.

A second foundational concept in Earth jurisprudence is the view that the Earth is an interconnected community and there is a *relationship-based existence* between

---

[23] See www.earthlaws.org.au.

[24] Burdon (2011).

[25] Pelizzon and Ricketts (2015).

humanity and the rest of the Earth Community. This contrasts with the current Western legal view that creates legal relationships among people, and between people and corporations, through constructs like property law, but commodifies and exploits all other aspects of the natural world.[26] By framing the natural world as a community, Earth jurisprudence imposes greater constraints on humanity's actions than our current legal system does. By claiming that 'the primary concern of the human community must be the preservation of the comprehensive community', Berry argued for a human world that works to ensure that all members of the Earth Community can thrive and continue their evolutionary journey.[27]

This concept of an 'Earth Community' is in some ways comparable to the Aboriginal legal system which is based on a relationist ethos. As outlined earlier in this book, Indigenous peoples' laws are built on the deep connection and relationist basis of human existence. However, as noted above, it is difficult to compare general statements in Earth jurisprudence to the ancient, specific, deep connection that Indigenous peoples have in practice. However, inviting Westerners to see the world as being made up of relationships is an important way to challenge them to rethink the deepest beliefs in their culture.

Third, many advocates of Earth jurisprudence have argued that the Earth Community and all the beings that constitute it have rights, including the right to exist, to habitat or a place to be and to participate in the evolution of the Earth Community.[28] Berry argued that 'nature's rights should be the central issue in any ... discussion of the legal context of our society'.[29] This view contrasts with the dominant approach in the Western legal system, which privileges and grants rights only to humans and selected human constructs, such as corporations or government entities. Granting Rights to Nature is a radical rethinking of the role of our anthropocentric legal system, yet the idea appears to be taking hold in many jurisdictions.

Berry distinguishes the Rights of Nature from other legal rights by saying they are 'analogous'[30]: that is, these rights are already existent; they are not created by human law but rather are created by the very act of the Universe bringing forth its evolutionary processes. These Rights of Nature come from the same source as human rights: the Universe itself.[31] Therefore, it is the work of Earth jurisprudence to develop and advocate for cultural, legal—and even spiritual change—that recognises these already existing 'rights' and provide legal consideration and protection of those rights.

---

[26] Cullinan, in Graham (2011).

[27] Ibid., Berry, p. 580.

[28] Berry (2002).

[29] Ibid. Berry, p. 80.

[30] Tuff, N. (n.d.). In *A Conversation with Thomas Berry*, Thomas Berry states "Everything has rights. How could everything have rights? Well, it's an analogy. A tree needs tree rights. A bird needs bird rights... To say that something exists is true, but not the same." Available at: http://www.humansandnature.org/.

[31] Ibid.

This articulation of rights is one of the areas in which Earth jurisprudence diverges from any comparable concepts in Aboriginal law. As outlined earlier in this book, Aboriginal laws are built upon a Custodial Ethic, the concept of reciprocity and what Mary Graham calls 'the law of obligation'. While certain people within Aboriginal communities have a right to certain aspects of knowledge and law, rights-based laws and the notion of any living thing having a 'right' are not a conceptual element in the Aboriginal legal system. Rights-based law is seen as a conflict-oriented approach to resolving different Land use demands. This contrasts with the fundamental goal of Aboriginal societies, which is to create stability, harmony and balance.

A further, fundamental problem with 'rights' is that they are seen as a distinctly Western legal concept, which have emerged from the colonial project and are strengthened by the international legal system created by—and used against First Nations Peoples by—colonial powers.[32] However despite these conceptual clashes, around the world there are many Indigenous peoples who are embracing the Rights of Nature concept and implementing or adopting Rights of Nature laws.[33] These groups see the Rights of Nature as a conceptual framework that can be used *within* Western law, to challenge fundamental principles *of* Western law such as private property rights that permit environmental destruction.

The recent legal developments in New Zealand, India, Colombia, Bangladesh, Mexico and other jurisdictions, that have seen legislation and court cases recognise rivers, forests and other living entities as having 'legal personhood' or being 'the subject of legal rights' and can be differentiated from jurisdiction-wide Rights of Nature laws, are in some cases much closer to some of the concepts of interrelationships in Aboriginal law. For example, Aotearoa/New Zealand's recognition of 'legal personhood' status for the Whanganui River, Urewera Forest and Taranaki Mountain, which have emerged from Settlement Agreements under the Treaty of Waitangi, are based on Māori Peoples' spiritual connection to these living ancestors and offer interesting and important connections between First Nations Peoples' laws and Western legal constructs.[34]

Some writers see Rights of Nature laws and Legal Personhood laws not as an end in themselves, but as *important building blocks between cultural and legal systems, that can support a transformation of Western law from human-centred to Earth-centred governance, that is appropriate to the culture and specific ecology of a place.* Rights of Nature and Legal Personhood laws offer a way for Westerners to see their own legal system differently, and to reconfigure Western laws, in order to start building a new jurisprudence of Earth-centred, relationist law. Where appropriate, and with the

---

[32] Irene Watson, op. cit., p. 7.

[33] For example, see the decision by the Ho-Chunk Tribe in the USA in 2016 to adopt Rights of Nature in their Constitution. Available at: https://celdf.org/2016/09/press-release-ho-chunk-nation-general-council-approves-rights-nature-constitutional-amendment/; also see the statement by the Ponca First Nations in 2018. Available at: http://indigenousagain.com/first-tribe-u-s-recognizes-rights-nature-law/.

[34] For a brief overview of Rights of Nature and legal personhood laws around the world, see Maloney (2018).

permission and leadership of First Nations Peoples, such laws can also offer a legal and conceptual 'bridge' between First Nations laws and Western laws.

In Australia, we are seeing some Indigenous peoples using the 'framing' of Rights of Nature in documents, statements and initiatives. In 2016, people in the Western Australian region now known as the Kimberley created an historic declaration—the Fitzroy River Declaration—which sets out their intention to protect and manage the River, and recognises that 'the River is a living ancestral being and has a right to life'.[35]

Further work by Anne Poelina, Donna Bagnall and others (discussed elsewhere in this book) outline the important framing of 'legal rights for ancestral beings' as a key strategy for protecting sacred places such as the Martuwarra River.

In 2017, sixteen Aboriginal nations from across the northern Murray-Darling Basin signed a Treaty to work together, and have a united voice, on issues of importance to them.[36] The Treaty, known as the Union of Sovereign First Nations of the Northern Murray-Darling Basin, includes a pledge to uphold the 'rights of Mother Earth', as follows:

> The rights of Mother Earth are upheld by all Nations …. And we pledge our commitment to ensuring 'respect' and preservation of her inalienable rights and all things natural. We acknowledge that these guarantees are the absolute inherent rights to the human condition.[37]

In 2017, the Victorian government passed the *Yarra River Protection (Willip-gin Birrarung Murron)* Act, which enables the identification of the Yarra River and the many hundreds of parcels of public Land it flows through as one living, integrated natural entity for protection and improvement. While this legislation does not change the legal status of the river, or explicitly refer to the Rights of Nature, its acknowledgement of the river as a living entity is important in Australian law, and it's the first time in Australia that Aboriginal language and custodial responsibilities are recognised in connection to and responsibility for this important waterway.[38]

A fourth, and important element, of Earth jurisprudence is the idea of Earth Democracy. Many advocates for the Rights of Nature embed Nature rights within a framework of 'Earth Democracy'. Earth Democracy has been defined as an attempt to fuse eco-centric ethics with deeper forms of human democracy and public participation.[39] It promotes the idea that all human and non-human life forms are borne of Earth, and as evolutionary companions, we all have a right to exist, thrive and evolve. In terms of *human* relationships, Earth Democracy is a concept that examines power, privilege and inequity, and rejects them in favour of the idea that all people have the right to their own self-determination, particularly when it comes to Earth stewardship within their local communities.

---

[35] See Martuwarra Fitzroy River Council (2016).

[36] See Wainwright (2017).

[37] See Union of Sovereign First Nations of the Northern Murray-Darling Basin (2017).

[38] Yarra River Protection (Wilip-gin Birrarung murron) Act 2017. Available at: https://www.water.vic.gov.au/waterways-and-catchments/protecting-the-yarra/yarra-river-protection-act.

[39] Burdon (2015).

It is important to recognise that under an Earth jurisprudence approach, human rights and 'democracy' are an interdependent and correlative subset of Earth rights; humanity cannot be healthy and secure if Earth is veering towards depletion and over-extraction.

From an Earth laws perspective, the idea of Earth Democracy is an important one for Westerners to embrace and some elements of the concept resonates with Aboriginal law. Aboriginal law is built on deep respect for each other's autonomy; it is non-hierarchical, and governance structures exist to separate power and authority so that power is diffused throughout the community. Consequently, notions of Earth Democracy—particularly when articulated as including an obligation to care for your local environment and local place—can be seen as important for Westerners, so that they take responsibility for their impact on Country.

The idea that a small elite could control the rest of a community was unheard of in Aboriginal society. Everyone has an equal value in society, and everyone has an obligation to care for Country and for one another. When a controlling ethic or spiritual basis emerges in a society that prioritises ego over community, or the individual over the collective, then the journey to societal and spiritual hierarchies begins, and unfairness and injustice follow.

It is the notion of Earth Democracy, and local communities' claims for ecological and social justice, that is driving some initial Rights of Nature campaigns in Australia. The Rights of Nature concept is receiving increasing attention from non-Indigenous communities in Australia, and to date, all non-Indigenous communities interested in the Rights of Nature are first engaging with First Nations Peoples to explore how such concepts might (or might not) be used by people working together in a local region.

Since 2018, we have seen a number of community-driven initiatives that reflect how Rights of Nature can capture peoples' imagination in a way that traditional environmental law does not, and how Rights of Nature framing and strategies can be embraced by people seeking to support Earth Democracy.

In March 2018, more than 100 local people rallied in support of the Margaret River, in Western Australia.[40] Their signs, banners and strategy focused on giving the river its own voice and its own legal rights. One of the local advocates for rights of the river said that people 'understood the idea of recognising the river as a living entity, because we all know it's more than just a resource, it's alive and it has a right to exist'.[41] In 2019, Diane Evers, MP in the Western Australian parliament, introduced a Rights of Nature law for Western Australia, to stimulate conversation and debate about the destruction of nature in that state.

In April 2021, the Blue Mountains City Council (BMCC) became the first Local Council—and in fact the first Government entity—in Australia, to embed 'Rights of Nature' as a keystone concept into its operational practices, planning process and advocacy program. On 27 April 2021, the Council unanimously resolved to proceed

[40] Lynch (2018).

[41] Personal Communication, 24 March 2018.

with a new program of action that will see Rights of Nature concepts inform its long-term planning and operational activities.

The innovative approach was developed in response to a resolution passed by an Ordinary Meeting of the BMCC on 31 March 2020. The Council will begin its program by hosting community workshops and in-depth discussions with Indigenous and non-Indigenous peoples across the Blue Mountains, to explore what Rights of Nature and other eco-centric concepts mean for the people and economies of the region.

Implications of Emerging 'Earth Laws'

Earth laws also offers an important foundation for exploring new collaborations between Indigenous and non-Indigenous communities in Australia and the Pacific, as it offers a framework that can bring people together around the common themes of Caring for Country and the Relationist Ethos, and open up dialogue about 'legal rights for ancestral beings', legal pluralism and other innovative legal approaches.

4.1.3 Acknowledge Indigenous Sovereignty and Privilege First Laws

Through the Indigenous Think Tank, we explore a pathway for our Nation and affirm the need to engage with the issue of sovereignty for First Nations Peoples.

As discussed above, 'integrating' Indigenous laws and rights into existing Western law is one of the most accepted ways for Western legal systems to support Indigenous peoples, as it still assumes the dominance of Western laws and institutions. It could be suggested that 'sovereignty' is at the other end of the spectrum, as it is much more complex and difficult for Western law—and Western societies—to understand and engage with.

Indigenous sovereignty is, for many Western commentators and community members, confusing and contentious. For some it challenges Western notions of absolute sovereignty and territorial integrity. For others, it connects with Indigenous self-determination and can be flexible in its meaning.

Indigenous peoples in the Arctic noted in their 'Circumpolar Inuit Declaration on Sovereignty in the Arctic' that:

> "Sovereignty" is a term that has often been used to refer to the absolute and independent authority of a community or nation both internally and externally. Sovereignty is a contested concept, however, and does not have a fixed meaning. Old ideas of sovereignty are breaking down as different governance models, such as the European Union, evolve. Sovereignties overlap and are frequently divided within federations in creative ways to recognise the right of peoples. For Inuit living within the states of Russia, Canada, the USA and Denmark/ Greenland, issues of sovereignty and sovereign rights must be examined and assessed in the context of our long history of struggle to gain recognition and respect as an Arctic indigenous

> people having the right to exercise self-determination over our lives, territories, cultures and languages.[42]

In Australia, Dominic O'Sullivan noted in 2018, that:

> Much of the controversy stems from overstated assumptions of what sovereignty means. In practical terms, sovereignty is not the absolute, indivisible and incontestable power that Thomas Hobbes made it in Leviathan. Sovereignty is not an authority that has to belong either exclusively with the Crown or exclusively with Indigenous nations … Sovereignty, with all its interpretations and misinterpretations, is the point on which disagreement is most likely to occur {regarding treaty negotiations}. It is the source of the disagreements most likely to expose irreconcilable differences as the negotiations proceed.[43]

One of the clearest statements about the complexities around Indigenous sovereignty was made by Worimi man Dr. William (Bill) Jonas AM, in 2002, and is set out below.

Aboriginal Sovereignty—Excerpts from Speech by Dr. William (Bill) Jonas AM

To date, Aboriginal sovereignty has tended to be defined as something analogous to the sovereignty of the State or government in international law. It has, in my opinion, been wrongly conflated with the concept of 'State sovereignty'.

This conflation privileges non-Indigenous interpretations and understandings of sovereignty over Indigenous ones in a way that pre-determines the outcome … It establishes a framework in which Aboriginal sovereignty is pitted against the existing system. Aboriginal sovereignty becomes an oppositional force. It becomes a threat to territorial integrity; to our system of government; to our way of life. And as a consequence, it irresistibly leads the broader community to the conclusion that Aboriginal sovereignty cannot be recognised and must be resisted.

First, we need to re-conceptualise and define Aboriginal sovereignty. It needs to be understood by the broader community that it is not a threat to State sovereignty, but in fact an enhancement of that sovereignty and something of mutual benefit. It must be accepted that Aboriginal sovereignty is inter-related with State sovereignty rather than in opposition or competition with it. Until this distinction can be understood in the broader community, we will continue to face political and legal dead-ends on the road to a treaty. In many ways this leads us away from a strictly legal conception of sovereignty to a political one.

Second, in considering how best we might do this, there needs to be consideration as to whether we should in fact call it Aboriginal sovereignty or re-name it something that is perhaps less threatening, or which more accurately reflects Indigenous aspirations. At this stage I don't advocate abandonment of calling it Aboriginal sovereignty. But I do think that we need to look to the ultimate end that we are seeking to achieve. We need not be precious about language. And we should bear in mind the danger that insisting on using 'sovereignty' could attract the wrong kind of attention - giving the government the excuse to focus on extinguishment or abandonment of sovereignty rather than its recognition.

Third, if we accept that it is illegitimate for government, and the courts, to seek to impose a definition of Aboriginal sovereignty, that leads us to accept also that the definition and scope of Aboriginal sovereignty is a matter entirely for Indigenous people, to be determined according to Indigenous systems of law and governance. The implication of this is that our efforts, as Indigenous people, should be directed to establishing the boundaries of our sovereignty. We must stop asking government to 'give us sovereignty'. It isn't the government's to give. You cannot be given

[42] A Circumpolar Inuit Declaration on Sovereignty in the Arctic, Para 2.1. Available at: https://www.itk.ca/circumpolar-declaration-arctic-soveriegnty/.

[43] *The Conversation*, https://theconversation.com/victorias-treaty-with-indigenous-peoples-must-address-vexed-questions-of-sovereignty-98758.

> *sovereignty, much as you cannot be given self-determination - you must claim it, define it and exercise it.*[44]

4.1.4 Legal Pluralism

The principle of 'legal pluralism', where multiple legal systems may co-exist, has the potential to provide a solid foundation for recognising and enforcing Indigenous sovereignty, tenure and governance.[45] Importantly, work by Donna Bagnall, one of the members of the Indigenous Think Tank that formed part of the authorship for this book, demonstrates that *the Australian legal system is already operating within a legal pluralism framework*. Her analysis can be found below, at Sect. 4.4.

4.2 Exploring Legal Pluralism as a Way Forward for Australia

Legal pluralism is a complex subject and draws from a large body of scholarship across several disciplines, from theoretical and conceptual discussions to applied case studies. Noting the inter-disciplinary nature of legal pluralism, Rohe et al., in their study of coastal fisheries governance in some Pacific Island nations, argue that there is a need for a greater degree of collaboration between disciplines (such as law and anthropology) in studies of legal pluralism.[46]

While this book is not an exhaustive exploration of legal pluralism, we do point to the many and varied ways in which the subject may be considered. As Tamanaha indicates, the term 'pluralism' itself 'simply means more than one, which can be applied to anything and framed at various levels of specificity and generality'.[47] He states of legal pluralism:

> The label legal pluralism has been used to refer to a plurality of interpretations of a single set of laws; to subsystems of law within a single system; to the same tribunals applying distinct bodies of law and separate tribunals applying different bodies of law within a system; to hybrid legal systems that grew out of the interaction between distinct bodies of law; to the coexistence of separate forms of law within a single society; to the coexistence of different subject matter regimes within international law; to the coexistence of multiple legal systems between and across states; and other variations. Each of these examples has been discussed in the literature on legal pluralism, though they are very different.[48]

Within its multidisciplinary frame, there are many dimensions to the concept of legal pluralism, including as it pertains to Indigenous peoples. One element for example,

---

[44] Jonas (2002).

[45] Fernandez-LLamazares et al. p. 156.

[46] Rohe et al. (2019).

[47] Tamanaha. (2021).

[48] Ibid.

concerns the power dynamics and tensions between diverse legal systems. Short, who examines legal pluralism in an Ecuadorian context, concludes that potential conflicts between state-based legal systems and Indigenous ones may be alleviated by enabling greater autonomy for Indigenous peoples to develop their own systems, in accordance with the United Nations Declaration on the Rights of Indigenous Peoples (UNDRIP).[49] This goes to questions of Indigenous self-determination, and balancing self-determining Indigenous communities and/or organisations, with State-based legal and political systems. The discussions throughout this book on Indigenous peoples' First Laws argue for recognition of these in the political systems of the nation state. In regards to self-determination and environmental rights, Eichler and Navarro explore the "procedural dimension underlying 'indigenous environmental rights', and the importance of collective and intergenerational rights in channelling indigenous environmental rights into dominant legal orders while facilitating the exercise of these rights".[50] They examine the concept of Indigenous environmental rights, the articulation of these in international law, and the potential that these rights have in considerations around bridging the human-nature divide, and in shaping a self-determining and legal pluralist approach within a decolonising frame. Thus:

> In that sense, indigenous environmental rights are being claimable by indigenous peoples procedurally speaking, they operate as facilitators to enforce claims on behalf of non-human species, they become articulated through broader collective and intergenerational rights, or as manifestations of legal pluralism. In that sense, we regard indigenous environmental rights as a *sui generis* matter, rather than placing the former under the broad umbrella of biodiversity regimes, environmental law or, alternatively, to find accommodation under dualistic frames. These dualistic manifestations become apparent in the anthropocentric vs.(?) eco-centric divide predominant in current thinking.[51]

Indigenous environmental rights may be envisaged as a type of group, or collective rights, which are important in the context of diverse forms of legal pluralism. They may be compared with what some writers are describing as 'biocultural rights', a form of group rights that can be interpreted from readings of the 2011 *Nagoya Protocol on Access and Benefit-Sharing*, an adjunct to the UN *Convention on Biological Diversity* (see discussion above in this book).[52] In this sense, Eichler and Navarro state that biocultural rights may be considered as distinct from Indigenous rights and do not "carry an undertone of political self-determination" and ultimately are not "necessarily based on ethnicity, religion or minority status".[53]

Among the many writers on legal pluralism are the Benda-Beckmanns, whose work sets the context for some of the essential theoretical and conceptual thinking

---

[49] Short. (2014).

[50] Eichlera and Navarro (2023), at p. 5.

[51] Ibid.

[52] On Indigenous biocultural rights see, for example, Girard et al. (2022). Marina Agar (2017), Bavikatte (2014).

[53] Eichler and Navarro, op. cit., p. 8, citing Bavikatte and Bennett (2015), at p. 27.

around this subject.[54] Their work is important to understand the historical, anthropological and ethnographic contexts to legal pluralism, the colonial and post-colonial situations, and the complex interplay between state, and non-state actors in the multiplicity of pluralist systems.

Yet another approach to legal pluralism comes from Helen Dancer, who calls for a "deep legal pluralism" that "both decentres anthropocentric thinking on the environment and decentres the state in the development of Earth law". This call is framed in the context of seeking a 'harmony' between humans and nature in the Anthropocene.[55]

In exploring the melding of different legal systems, it is also useful to consider another strand of thinking, in which the notions such as 'bridging' alternative knowledges and epistemologies, and what some writers have denoted as 'southern knowledge' or 'southern epistemologies'. De Sousa Santos is one writer whose work takes up this theme, as he theorises a shift away from top-down, Eurocentric and dominant paradigms, knowledges and epistemologies, to alternative ways of knowing and thinking. De Sousa Santos's work is influential in the project of seeking to strengthen Indigenous legal systems in plural frameworks.[56]

4.2.1 How Does Legal Pluralism Work? Hierarchies? Flat Structures?

The roles of traditional and customary legal systems are a subject that has engaged extensive observation, analysis and discussion in the ethnographic, anthropological and legal-anthropological literature. Much of the literature examines the complex relationships between law and society, and the vast array of diverse arrangements, both historically, and in the present day. One of the many challenges to establishing successful legal pluralism is to gain deeper understandings of the ways that different legal systems interact or engage, and the nexus between these, and social, political and economic systems. Further, in considering diverse, alternative legal systems such as Indigenous laws and customary approaches, the relationships between these, and the nation state in colonial-settler countries, are also subjects for discussion in the literature. Merry's 1988 review article sets out some of these issues. She notes that "As they documented the rich variety of social control, social pressure, custom, customary law, and judicial procedure within small-scale societies ... anthropologists gradually realized that colonized peoples had both indigenous law and European law".[57] She comments that 'legal pluralism goes far deeper than the joining of European and

[54] See, for example, von Benda-Beckmann (2002); See also von Benda-Beckmann and Turner (2018).

[55] Dancer (2021).

[56] De Sousa Santos, op. cit.

[57] Engle Merry (1988), p. 869.

traditional forms of law. We are only now beginning to explore the extent to which previously colonized societies are legally and culturally plural'.[58]

There is an extensive body of literature that explores plural legal systems in specific contexts of place, peoples and the governance of natural resources and ecosystems. Rohe et al., for example, discuss plural legal systems in regard to governance of coastal fisheries in Fiji and the Solomon Islands. Here, long-established customary rights in the management of, and regulation of access to, marine resources, form the basis for community-based management approaches.[59] These authors explore the dynamics that come into play with the intersection of these community and customary-based systems, and state-based regulatory legal systems. Their analysis highlights the diversity of situations of legal pluralism, and in the intersections between state, and non-state-based legal systems. These, they conclude, can range from 'indifference to accommodation and mutual support'.[60]

In considering the intersections between and among different legal systems, towards enabling a legal pluralism, we would argue that deep regard must be had for recognition and understanding of Indigenous legal systems and traditions. Taking into account the stories presented in this book, and wisdom from many Indigenous thinkers, writers and scholars, as well as extant literature, it can be said that Indigenous legal systems can be characterised by certain distinct features. These, in general, include an emphasis on connections between the human and the natural domains, and, in one description, 'norms that govern the maintenance of appropriate balance through differentiation and shared responsibility'. This point is elaborated:

> In many accounts, these norms have a strong emphasis on building and maintaining relationships, deliberation and persuasion, witness and observation, the maintenance of requisite affect and openness in the conduct of relationships, and a commitment to maintaining balance in the human, natural, and spiritual realms (these being in any case deeply entwined with one another).[61]

In her analysis of the relationships between Indigenous legal systems and majority legal systems in Commonwealth settler-colonial countries of Canada, Australia and New Zealand, Kirsty Gover makes a plea for recognition and acceptance of Indigenous law:

> The important scholarship of Indigenous legal scholars, along with their interventions in legal education and with the legal profession, are works of considerable generosity that show the operation of these traditions in practice. Legal pluralist approaches could support these efforts by encouraging settler attentiveness to the norms, values and processes that underpin externally observable indigenous law. This would bring us closer to a just and equitable relationship between settler and indigenous legal systems, premised on the legal traditions of both.[62]

---

[58] Ibid., p. 870.

[59] Rohe et al., op. cit.

[60] Rohe et al., op. cit., p. 96.

[61] Gover (2020), p. 875.

[62] Kirsty Gover, op. cit., p. 875.

There are many colonial-settler countries and other jurisdictions that have, or are beginning to recognise, Indigenous laws in some way. Borrows states that among these are many Pacific Island states, as well as South Africa, Peru, Bolivia, Columbia and Ghana.[63]

Donna Bagnall outlines below how the Australian legal system is in fact already a plural legal system.

4.3 Examples from the Pacific Region

The small island nations of the Pacific region present opportunities to examine diverse ways in which Western laws might be integrated with local Indigenous customary laws and practices. Techera, for example, sets out the context, drawing attention to the challenge of legal pluralism in situations with rapidly developing international environmental laws.[64] She states that '[T]he bulk of the states in the region have a long history of customary law and traditional governance mechanisms, as well as a Western (in most cases common law) legal system established during colonial times'.[65] Explaining further, she writes that:

> Whilst most of these countries have not yet suffered the worst environmental problems, they are facing many contemporary challenges including over-utilisation of Land and natural resources, urbanisation and pollution. In this context, identifying how international law can be implemented effectively at the national level, in ways which do not conflict with deeply held customary norms, is a complex task. In many SIDS [Small Island Developing States] the majority of indigenous people continue to live at least a partially traditional lifestyle which fits uneasily with Western legislative models. At the same time these countries are poorly resourced and often lack technical expertise to draft comprehensive legislation that implements international environmental obligations whilst addressing indigenous rights, local tradition and customary law. Therefore, appropriate legal strategies need to be identified which address both indigenous rights and environmental law outcomes.[66]

Pacific Island nations that have legislated to recognise pre-existing customary laws, either constitutionally and/or in statute law, include Cook Islands, Fiji, Kiribati, Tokelau, Marshall Islands, Nauru, Samoa, Tuvalu, Vanuatu and Papua New Guinea (see, for example, Borrows.)[67]

---

63 Borrows, op. cit., pp. 216–217.

64 Techera (2010), p. 172.

65 Ibid., p. 172.

66 Ibid.

67 Borrows, op. cit., p. 216.

4.3.1 Conflict of Laws

In Western legal systems, there is a body of law designed specifically to resolve conflicts between the application of different laws. Legal pluralism requires very careful institutional and legal structures, and if legal pluralism emerges in Australia, rules and structures will need to be put in place to facilitate the effective operation of different legal systems. In particular, careful attention would need to be paid to ensure Indigenous First Laws are not made subservient to Western laws.

The challenges and potential tensions between different legal systems for small Pacific Island states are noted by Techera, who discusses these with particular reference to human rights. She states that: 'not all indigenous customs and practices are environmentally beneficial and some can inhibit the realisation of human rights'.[68] Explaining further, she writes:

> Overcoming tensions between indigenous customary law and state-based legislation is therefore essential. This is particularly important in relation to the domestic implementation of international environmental law because of the close cultural and spiritual connection indigenous people have with nature and the wealth of traditional ecological knowledge (TEK) and customary law that has developed. A further challenge is that many customary laws and governance institutions have become eroded over time and may require revitalising or may no longer be viable.[69]

Drawing on the examples of legal pluralism in Pacific Island nations, as noted above, Techera argues that there should be more international attention given to exploring the many challenges and complexities in regard to the implementation of international laws in legally pluralist states.

The prevailing dominant state-based legal systems are, in a sense, 'blind', or 'blinkered' when it comes to their ability to recognise and incorporate alternative systems of laws, rights and values. One writer takes up this point, arguing that an 'emphasis on litigation' in post-colonial state-based legal systems, renders these latter unable to recognise, or to understand Indigenous peoples' rights and interests.[70] This 'invisibility' of Indigenous systems poses potential conflicts between state-based legal regimes and Indigenous laws in endeavours to formulate legal pluralistic approaches. Elsana argues that 'systemic structural change' is required in states' legal systems, to allow these state systems to 'see' and 'recognise' Indigenous rights, and to be able to 'adopt' Indigenous legal systems as 'another source for rights'.[71]

---

[68] Techera, op. cit., p. 173.

[69] Ibid.

[70] Elsana (2019).

[71] Ibid.

4.4 Australia Has Been Legally Pluralistic Since the *Mabo* Case—An Analysis of the Current Law and Future Possibilities—by Donna Bagnall

Donna Bagnall, a lawyer and member of the Indigenous Think Tank, has written an extensive analysis of legal pluralism in Australia.

Donna suggests that there 'are numerous signs that show us that Australia's legal system is already one that *should properly be operating in plurality with First Law but* is not fulfilling this mandate and duly implementing pre-existing customary laws and right.'

In her analysis, Donna discusses the case law and legal developments since the Mabo case, that demonstrate the Australian legal system is *actually already a plural* system. Her analysis contains four sections in which she explains:

(1) How First Law (native title) rights and interests must be rendered in their own terms;
(2) How First Laws, customs and rights, beyond Land-related rights, may continue to apply in Australia;
(3) There are two separate sources of Land title in Australia, but native title is subject to 'structural inequality';
(4) First Law rights and interests can be enforced in Equity.

Donna then discusses how the nation can create legal and institutional systems that implement legal pluralism.

Finally, Donna provides some reflections on the key messages from her analysis.

This section considers how we can create a truly plural legal system in Australia, with First Law (Indigenous customary law) and the Australian Western law[72] *working in tandem* to achieve a 'sustainable life' in Australia for First Peoples and for all Australian citizens under the Australian legal system. Indeed, the aim is for the Australian law in its totality, and in its plurality, to deliver a regenerative Country, a regenerative economy and a regenerative humanity. A humanity that is in essence revivified through the regeneration of its legal system.

This revivification (essentially a full renaissance) of our law and humanity needs to be one in which the 'Rule of Law' for both bodies of law is given 'full respect and full effect'. At present, the Australian legal system is sick. The Australian Western law has lost its way, its soul, its principles and its values. It needs some core principles restored, and some ancient wisdom in the form of ethics and equity to restore it to good health, akin to a dose of 'bush medicine'. Meanwhile, First Law has been cast aside and pushed 'outback', as if it was sent on a metaphorical walkabout for the

[72] The Australian Western law is a descriptor used here to refer to the Australian law including the common law and statutory law of the Commonwealth and the States of Australia.

past 233 years, because now is the time for it to return with its ancient wisdom and take up its rightful place as an Elder and a steward of the Australian legal system.

4.5 What Are the Signs that the Australian Legal System Is *Actually Plural* but Not Being Implemented?

There are numerous signs that show us that Australia's legal system is already one that *should properly be operating in plurality with First Law* (but is not fulfilling this mandate and duly implementing pre-existing customary laws and rights).

1. First Law (native title) rights and interests must be rendered in its own terms

Mabo (No. 2)[73]

Brennan J in the High Court judgement (6:1 majority) held:

- "***Native title has its origin in and is given its content by the traditional laws*** acknowledged by and the traditional customs observed by the indigenous inhabitants of a territory. The ***nature and incidents*** of native title ***must be ascertained as a matter of fact by reference to those laws and customs***." [64]
- "...Australian law can protect the interests of members of an indigenous clan or group, whether communally or individually, only in conformity with the traditional laws and customs of the people to whom the clan or group belongs and only where members of the clan or group acknowledge those laws and observe those customs (so far as it is practicable to do so)." [66]
- "...native title, being recognised by the common law ***may be protected by such legal or equitable remedies as are appropriate*** to the particular rights and interests established by the evidence, whether proprietary or personal and usufructuary in nature and whether possessed by a community, a group or an individual." [68]
- "The ***incidents of a particular native title*** relating to ...the grouping of persons to possess rights and interests in Land are ***matters to be determined by the laws and customs of the indigenous inhabitants,*** provided those laws and customs are not so repugnant to natural justice, equity and good conscience that judicial sanctions under the new regime must be withheld." [68]

Fortescue Metals[74]—All five Justices of the Full Federal Court (FFC) unanimously confirmed that:

- "The very foundation of traditional Aboriginal law and customs ...***is in the spiritual, and the intermingling of the spiritual with the physical, with people and with Land. That is how Aboriginal law works***." [288]

---

[73] *Mabo v Queensland (No. 2)* [1992] HCA 23 *(Mabo (No. 2))*, per Mason CJ, Brennan, Deane, Toohey, Gaudron, and McHugh JJ. Dawson J dissenting.

[74] *Fortescue Metals Group v Warrie on behalf of the Yindjibarndi People* [2019] FCAFC 177; BC201909419 "Fortescue Metals".

- "The distinctions … between spiritual belief and real property rights, or personal property rights, are not to be imported into an assessment of the existence and content of aboriginal customary law. ***To do so would be to destroy the fabric of that customary law***." [emphasis added] [288]
- "…***the spiritual relationship*** of Aboriginal people to their country is ***enmeshed in traditional law and custom***, and that is one of the matters which distinguishes the traditional laws and customs of Aboriginal people from common law proprietary rights." [361]
- "…one starts with identification, through evidence, of the content of traditional law and custom, and then asks to what rights and interests relating to Land that law and custom gives rise. Only then does the Court, having identified those rights and interests, look for how those rights should be ***recognised, or translated***, by reference to Anglo-Australian law." [363]
- "…if what the Court finds, on the evidence, is traditional laws requiring permission to be granted to strangers to enter or exploit country, with the purposes of those laws being both to protect country and to protect transgressors from harm, then this may be properly characterised as a ***right to control access, which is the essence of exclusive possession***." [363]
- "…it is to misunderstand the concept of native title rights and interests to require them to fit into non-Aboriginal concepts of property, the exercise of proprietary rights and the enforcement of property rights. …That is why what occurs is ***recognition*** of native title; not conferral, and ***not transformation*** into non-Aboriginal property rights." [287–288]
- "…the assessment and determination of the content of the traditional laws and customs of any given claim group, and the rights and interests relating to Land to which those laws and customs give rise, is an exercise performed within the universe of traditional law and custom. It is not dependent on proof of exercise against non-Aboriginal people (although such evidence may exist and may be especially relevant to matters such as continuity… nor is it dependent on effectiveness of enforcement against non-Aboriginal people. Indeed, the authorities make clear that ***it is more usual for traditional law to be treated as ineffectual, and this is what the Native Title Act is designed to remedy***." [286]
- "It would be an intolerable irony if post-sovereignty authorities and non-Aboriginal peoples whose society has been responsible for the dispossession and oppression of Aboriginal peoples were able to use the inability of those peoples to enforce their customary law against those who entered and sought to exploit their Land as a basis to continue the disenfranchisement. The objectives of the *Native Title Act* are not served by such an approach and nor do they countenance it." [290]

Therefore, one of the most important reasons why native title is *sui generis* ('of its own kind' and unique) is because '[n]ative title has its origin in and is given its content by the traditional laws acknowledged by and the traditional customs observed by the indigenous inhabitants of a territory'. This means that 'the ***nature and incidents*** of native title ***must be ascertained as a matter of fact by reference to those laws and customs***'.[75]

I believe that the full potential of this important point has been largely substantively missed in the Australian native title jurisprudence since it was enunciated in *Mabo (No.2)*, despite being often expressed. This is one critical proposition that establishes First Law as substantively *plural* with Western law in the Australian legal system.

The statements by the FFC in *Fortescue Metals* as set out above also provide emphatic reinforcement of this proposition, which means that native title should be rendered in customary law terms.[76]

As such, there is an opportunity to become bolder in asking the courts to recognise native title in a manner that is more authentic to customary law or First Law. and which is aligned with Indigenous world views, ontologies, and epistemologies. In this way, native title rights and interests could be rendered in accordance with the spiritual or metaphysical terms of the ancient First Law Songlines or Jukurrpa (Dreamings), such as recognising the existence of ancestral living beings within the Lands and waters, because that is the rich 'fabric' of the customary law and that is the character of the rights and interests possessed.[77]

Jagot and Mortimer JJ confirmed that 'it all depends on the evidence', illuminating that '[t]here are not necessarily any hard boundary lines, or prohibitions on how rights and interests might be articulated, and many nuances in terms of the nature and content of rights in Land and waters are possible'.[78]

In New Zealand, the Waitangi Tribunal decision in the Whanganui River case[79] provides a clear Antipodean authority for the proposition that 'native title must be rendered in its own terms' under the common law based on a long line of precedents going back to the Privy Council. The judgement provides a landmark precedent that brings to life its meaning in a very real and tangible way.

In that case, the Tribunal held that:

> [t]he conceptual understanding of the river as a Tupuna or ancestor emphasises the Māori thought that the river exists as a single and undivided entity or essence. Rendering the native title in its own terms, then, what Atihaunui owned was a river, not a bed, and a river entire, not dissected into parts.[80]

Accordingly, the Tribunal held that 'the interest of the Whanganui iwi in the River, their tupuna awa [ancestor], is more extensive than the attributes of ownership according to English legal notions', and that, 'the Whanganui iwi are entitled to benefit from the River and exercise authority in relation to it as its guardians for future generations'.[81]

---

[75] *Mabo (No. 2)*, per Brennan J, op. cit.

[76] Bagnall (2020a, 2020b). Fortescue Metals' application for special leave to appeal to the High Court against the Full Federal Court's decision was rejected by the High Court on 29 May 2020.

[77] Ibid.

[78] Fortescue Metals Group, op. cit.

[79] Tribunal (1999).

[80] Ibid., p. 337.

[81] Ibid., p. 375.

While we have not seen judicial decisions in Australia that have been as faithful to this requirement to 'render native title in its own terms' as that on display in the *Whanganui River* case,[82] the opportunity is nevertheless there for Australian lawyers to put this element of the doctrine of native title forward to the Australian courts. If we identify and expressly seek to have native title rendered in line with its sui generis character and incidents, and we request it to be rendered in line with the traditional laws and customs as established by the evidence, then we could expect to see 'new life breathed into native title' in Australia.[83]

In my view, this approach is required as a matter of law, not policy or ideology, under the common law doctrine of native title and is, therefore, itself a skeletal principle of the common law, particularly in a country such as Australia to whom the doctrine of *terra nullius* does not apply and which regards itself as 'settled but inhabited' despite no treaty having been agreed.[84]

Australian lawyers and judges, in failing to demand and give effect to this principle, would arguably be erring at law, as well as selling the doctrine of native title short of its unique power and potential to deliver appropriate outcomes to our nations' Indigenous owners. These outcomes could include, as occurred in the *Whanganui River* case,[85] the establishment of water co-stewardship rights that are aligned with fulfilling Indigenous guardianship responsibilities under regional governance models.

I have researched and collaborated closely with Professor Anne Poelina on the Martuwarra (Fitzroy River) in the Kimberley, WA, examining the River Law (*Warloongarriy* Law) of the Martuwarra and its significance by close analogy to the *Whanganui River* precedent, given the similar facts and common law native title principles applicable. We co-authored an article[86] on new legal pathways to fully recognise the rights of the River and the native title rights and interests of the Traditional Custodians that reflect 'First Law' epistemologies and ontologies of the Martuwarra as embodying a Living Ancestral being. This concept of 'ancestral beinghood' would recognise the River in terms of how the Martuwarra Traditional Custodians view the River, as being and embodying a living ancestor, the Rainbow Serpent creator being, one whole integrated living entity from source to sea, with a right to life and a right to flow.[87] This would also give effect to traditional law regional governance under *Wunan* Law, and guardianship rights and duties so as to

[82] Ibid.

[83] Gray (2002), Paper presented at the Australasian Law Teachers' Association Annual Conference, Perth, 29 Sept to 2 Oct, 62.

[84] Refer to *Mabo (No. 2)*, op. cit. Brennan J's discussion of terra nullius, and the native title doctrine where 'settled', 'conquered', or 'ceded'.

[85] Minister for Treaty of Waitangi Negotiations (2012). See also, *Te Awa Tupua (Whanganui River Claims Settlement) Bill*, available at: https://www.parliament.nz/en/pb/bills-and-laws/bills-proposed-laws/document/00DBHOH_BILL68939_1/te-awa-tupua-whanganui-river-claims-settlement-bill.

[86] RiverOfLife et al., op. cit.

[87] RiverOfLife et al., op. cit.

enable negotiation of co-stewardship arrangements with the WA government.[88] The Traditional Custodians who hold native title along the River (Yi-Martuwarra nations) collaborate and act jointly "to protect the globally significant spiritual, cultural, environmental, and scientific values of the River. This Indigenous authority comes from a deep relationship with Country, responsible for maintaining spiritual wellbeing and generating sustainable livelihoods and lifeways on Country: [Yi-Martuwarra] hold the right to practice [their] Law and spirituality in co-existence, peace, harmony, and balance with [their] sacred serpent ancestral being, *Yoongoorrookoo*, which formed Martuwarra".[89] As Professor Poelina conveys earlier in the book, *Yoongoorrookoo*, the Rainbow Serpent spiritual lifeforce lives within and is co-substantial with the River, and Yi-Martuwarra, the People 'who belong to the River', have an obligation to care for it.

The Traditional Custodians consider that the Martuwarra is best described as a spritual 'ancestral being', a legal subject that possesses legal rights. This is different from the legal subject of 'personhood', as the Traditional Custodians do not see the River as a person, but a physical and metaphysical (spiritual) non-human ancestor.[90] Under First Law, the River is already an entity, so it does not need to be incorporated as an entity using Western law, but rather simply recognised in terms of its own First Law.[91]

While not a native title case, it has also been exciting to see the Thalanyji Traditional Owners assert their First Law in the context of Aboriginal heritage laws. They argued that the construction of ten weirs on the Mindurru (Ashburton River) would mean that the water snake or Rainbow Serpent (Warnamankura) would be blocked from moving or could be harmed or killed, and this would destroy their sacred sites and songlines.[92]

Significantly, the State Administrative Tribunal (WA) has now handed down its landmark decision in this case (the *Ashburton River* case[93]), accepting the evidence of the Thalanyji people, and affirming the Minister's decision to refuse the consent under the *Aboriginal Heritage Act 1972 (WA)*.

The Tribunal's reasoning illuminates the legitimate place of First Law in the Australian legal context, and provides the clearest illustration yet of how it can be integrated, weaved or embedded into the Australian law so that it functions in substantive plurality with the common law. Specifically, the Tribunal found at [603–616] that:

---

[88] RiverOfLife et al., op. cit.

[89] Martuwarra, RiverOfLife, Poelina A, McDuffie M, Perdrisat M (2023) Martuwarra Fitzroy River Watershed: One society, one river law. PLOS Water 2(9): at page 9, e0000104. https://doi.org/10.1371/journal.pwat.0000104

[90] O'Donnell et al. (2020).

[91] Ibid.

[92] Collard (2021).

[93] Forrest and Forrest Pty Ltd and Minister for Aboriginal Affairs [2023] WASAT 28, per Pritchard, Willey and Barton.

1. "The Thalanyji people's relationship to the River is properly regarded as deeply spiritual", and "their beliefs in the water snake, which lives in the River, and which controls the natural flow of the River, are a central part of their spiritual beliefs in relation to the River." [603]
2. "The River is a place which is sacred to the Thalanyji people, given its central role in their spiritual beliefs, including the fact that it is where the water snake lives." [603]
3. "In the Thalanyji culture, the River is regarded with deep respect and reverence, and for that reason, we have found that the River is sacred to the Thalanyji people." [604]
4. "To interfere with the natural flow of the River (as will be the inevitable effect of the [project] will interfere in a significant way with a central tenet of the Thalanyji people's spiritual beliefs." [606]
5. "The preservation of Aboriginal culture, through the preservation of sites of importance and significance to Aboriginal people, is an important aspect of the preservation of the cultural heritage of the State." [613]
6. "Interfering with the natural flow of the River will cause spiritual harm to the Thalanyji people, by virtue of their concern that the water snake may die or leave the River, or become angry, and because the Thalanyji people will feel that they have failed in their duty as the custodians of the River." [613]
7. "The [project] would alter the River and the pools in it, because it would necessarily alter the natural flow of the River. To implement the [project] would therefore be to alter the River as an Aboriginal site." [614]
8. "The permanent effect of the [project] weighs strongly against the grant of consent." [616]

The Tribunal cited *Love*'s case in which Kiefel CJ (High Court) observed that the nature of the connection to Land and waters ascertained by reference to traditional laws and customs has been described as being not only material or physical, but also spiritual and cultural [199].

First Law is alive and well on Country, being acknowledged, practised, exercised and defended by the First Peoples in Western Australia, and validated and implemented by the judiciary.

2. First laws, customs and rights, beyond Land-related rights, may continue to apply in Australia

Love's case

The leading Australian precedent that illustrates how First Peoples' laws, customs and rights beyond Land-related rights may continue to apply in Australia is *Love*'s case.[94]

In *Love*'s case, the High Court held (4:3 majority) that 'Aboriginal Australians' (understood according to the tripartite test in *Mabo [No 2]*) are not within the reach of the 'aliens' power conferred by s 51(xix) of the Constitution' [81].

[94] Love v Commonwealth of Australia; Thoms v Commonwealth of Australia [2020] HCA 3.

Bell J, who led the majority decision, reasoned that:

> The position of Aboriginal Australians, … is sui generis. Notwithstanding the amplitude of the power conferred by s 51(xix), it does not extend to treating an Aboriginal Australian as an alien **because,** despite the circumstance of birth in another country, **an Aboriginal Australian cannot be said to belong to another place.** [74]

Gordon J stated her rationale for this succinctly: ***'Aboriginal Australians occupy a unique or sui generis position in this country***, such that they are not aliens'. [333].

Kiefel CJ (dissenting) considered that Aboriginal customary law 'did not apply beyond those limits' of Land-related rights in *Mabo* (*No.* 2) [29].

However, the majority decision confirms that the opposite is true, i.e. as Gordon J put it, '…***the tendency to think only in terms of native title rights and interests must be curbed***' [363].

Gordon J explained that 'Native title is ***one legal consequence flowing from common law recognition of the connection between Aboriginal Australians and the Land and waters*** that now make up Australia. ***That Aboriginal Australians are not 'aliens'*** within the meaning of that constitutional term in s 51(xix) ***is another***' [364].

Bell J used particularly strong words in his reasoning, stating that:

> **It is not offensive,** in the context of contemporary international understanding, **to recognise the cultural and spiritual dimensions of the distinctive connection** between indigenous peoples and their traditional Lands, and in light of that recognition **to hold that the exercise of the sovereign power of this nation does not extend to the exclusion of the indigenous inhabitants from the Australian community**. [73]

In a similar way, First Law emanates from Country, therefore the Law itself is part of Country and is connected with Country. As First Law itself is part of and connected with Country, there may be legitimate arguments that First Law's *sui generis* Songlines, Jukurrpa, totemic systems and other laws for maintaining them cannot lawfully be excluded or exiled from the Australian continent, any more than the Aboriginal and Torres Strait Islander Peoples themselves can be excluded or exiled from the Australian community.

Viewed in this way, First Laws are, in essence, the Constitution and By-laws from the Lands and waters. That is, they are the 'Earth Constitution' which cannot be repealed or expelled from Australia as 'alien' law. First Laws have the same origin and connection to the Land as the People themselves; therefore, it is strongly arguable that these Songlines, Jukurrpa, totemic systems and customs may never be extinguished.

Mabo (No. 2)

In *Mabo (No. 2)*, the High Court introduced a 'new class of settled colony at common law: a settled, yet legally inhabited, colony'.[95]

In reaching this classification, the High Court equated both the 'occupation of' and the 'settlement of' an inhabited territory with the 'occupation of' and the 'settlement of' an uninhabited territory for the purpose of legitimising the *acquisition*

[95] Secher (2005).

of sovereignty in international law and *in ascertaining the law of the territory* on colonisation at common law, respectively.[96]

The High Court challenged the notion that Australia was classified as 'acquired by occupation' as the basis for sovereignty, however as this was not justiciable, the High Court had to accept it.[97]

In relation to the basis on which Australia ascertained the law of the territory, by contrast, the High Court could determine the body of law that applied following sovereignty. The majority justices rejected the doctrine of *terra nullius* and applied the doctrine of *continuity pro tempore* to the settled but legally inhabited Lands, which means the existing law continued to apply for the time being, however, it applied only to Land rights. As such, other legal rights were immediately subjected to English common law, under the conventional doctrine of reception.[98]

Accordingly, the rationale underlying the *Mabo* decision cannot support the recognition of non-land rights of Aboriginal inhabitants in a settled colony.[99]

However, the legal finding that Australia was 'settled' but legally inhabited nevertheless leads to unexplored and open questions around the 'settlement' that the High Court found to exist as a matter of fact and law. The colonisation did not involve a cession (ceding sovereignty) with a Treaty, such as the Crown has argued occurred under the Treaty of Waitangi with the New Zealand Māori. Nor did the High Court equate the colonisation with the Lands being conquered.

In either of these two scenarios—cession or conquered Lands—the common law doctrine of continuity that applies means *that all customary laws continue to apply, unless contrary to common law concepts of justice and morality, or they are altered by the Crown.*[100] This applies to all laws, not just those relating to Land. In the case of cession, the continuing customary laws are also subject to the terms of the treaty of cession.[101]

It seems to me, just as the High Court was uncertain that sovereignty could be acquired by 'occupation' in Australia's circumstances,[102] it is equally uncertain and questionable to equate Australia's colonisation with the settlement of uninhabited Lands, rather than equating them with conquer. Indeed, the High Court's basis for adopting this view almost 30 years ago involved applying English law from 1889 (almost 100 years earlier) which was said to apply where the Lands were viewed as 'a tract of territory practically unoccupied, without settled inhabitants or settled law, at the time when it was peacefully annexed to the British dominions'.[103]

---

[96] Ibid.

[97] Ibid.

[98] Ibid.

[99] Ibid.

[100] Hepburn (2005). Melbourne University Law Review 1. Available at: http://classic.austlii.edu.au/au/journals/MelbULawRw/2005/1.html.

[101] Ibid.

[102] Secher, op. cit.

[103] *Cooper v. Stuart* (1889).

By today's standards, this view of the historical truth for Australia appears no more tenable than was the offensive doctrine of an enlarged notion of *terra nullius*. Therefore, it should similarly be rejected and overturned.

Even if the 'settled but legally inhabited' classification is maintained, then the notion of 'settlement' in the context of such extensively legally inhabited Lands takes on a whole new meaning in any event.

To my mind, questions that arise in the novel context of Australia being 'settled whilst legally inhabited' include what would be the ***implied terms*** of such an inferred settlement in an occupied territory with settled inhabitants and settled law, at the time when it was annexed with force to the British dominions?

The High Court, when asked this question, arguably would have little choice but to decide to legally equate the colonisation with 'conquer'/cession (treaty) by either overturning the 'settlement' classification, or, imputing terms/equitable principles into the 'settlement' of the laws that give effect to the Crown's honour and good conscience—***i.e. implied terms or equitable undertakings by the Crown that are no less favourable to the Indigenous inhabitants than those that would have applied had the Lands been conquered or ceded***. This is on the basis that the Aboriginal peoples legally inhabiting the continent at the time of 'settlement' and having extensive substantive proprietary Land rights (now retrospectively recognised) would not have endorsed 'settling' the law relating to their remaining laws and customs on terms that were any more detrimental than would have applied had their territories been conquered or ceded.

As such, in my view, determining the question of how the law was settled on a legally inhabited continent would necessarily involve (again retrospectively) imputing *an understanding* as *between* the First Peoples and the would-be settlers as to the *minimum implied terms* on the continuity of laws in a way that is aligned with the honour of the Crown and the high equitable principles developed by and applied by the Court of Chancery in England and its colonies.

In *Restoule v Canada*[104] 2018, the Ontario Superior Court of Justice considered the Anishinaabe First Nation's argument that the principle of the honour of the Crown, and the principles of treaty interpretation and rectification supported the claim for an implied term indexing the annuity payable under the Robinson-Huron Treaties, regardless of the subjective intention of the parties.

Justice Hennessy held that there was a mandatory and reviewable obligation to increase the annuity amount. While the Treaties included a provision for the annuity to be augmented 'from time to time', it was not just a discretion. Justice Hennessy considered the augmentation clause meant that the economic circumstances would trigger an increase to the annuities if the net Crown resource-based revenues permitted the Crown to increase the annuities without incurring a loss.

The forward-looking nature of the Treaties meant that it was unnecessary to imply the term. Rather, her Honour ruled that 'the principle of the honour of the Crown', and the Crown's fiduciary duty (a form of equitable obligation) imposed on the Crown the obligation to diligently implement the Treaties' promise to achieve their purpose.

---

[104] *Restoule v Canada* (Attorney General), 2018 ONSC 7701.

Their purpose was one of reflecting the value of the territories in the annuities and the agreement was relational and incorporated the concept of sharing of the Land.[105]

In a similar vein, in Australia, based on an ***honourable, equitable and forward-looking*** application of the common law doctrines to the scenario of a 'legally inhabited settlement' (or based on a truthful acknowledgement that Australia was not settled), it is arguable that in an appropriate case, the High Court could find that the doctrine of *continuity pro tempore* applies in Australia to all customary laws, not just laws relating to Land as was the focus in *Mabo (No.2)*.

In addition to the above potential, there is existing authority in the Australian common law, in *Mason v Tritton* (Kirby P) that Aboriginal law or custom can be a valid source of legal rights if it satisfies four requirements. The fourth of these requirements is that the right claimed is sought to be relied on in the exercise of traditional Aboriginal laws and customs.[106]

While there have been a number of cases refusing to apply the '*Mabo* principle' to recognise Aboriginal law, beyond rights and interests in Land,[107] at the same time, there have also been cases which provide judicial precedent for recognising non-land-related Aboriginal law, such as in *Goodsell v Yunupingu* (Gillies SM). The reasons for recognising the rights of Mr. Yunupingu to enforce Yolngu law on Yolngu Land included that: '*The use of Land* includes the enforcement of laws on that native Land applicable to and accepted by the natives on that Land who have a connection with that Land; that is, those people who are part of the Land'.[108]

Mr. Yunupingu, a Yolngu Elder, was found not guilty of assault, property damage, and theft after he objected to a photographer taking photographs without permission of Mr. Yunupingu's family in breach of Yolngu law. When he unsuccessfully attempted to settle the dispute, Yunupingu grabbed the camera from the photographer, removed the film and returned the camera. The not guilty ruling was based on the finding that Mr. Yunupingu's actions were 'done, made or caused in the exercise of a right recognised at law', and therefore were authorised under section 26(1)(a) of the *Criminal Code Act 1997* (NT).

Gillies SM held that Mr. Yunupingu's right to act under Yolngu law on the Land was recognised by, and enforceable under, the *Aboriginal Land Rights (Northern Territory) Act 1976* (Cth) as the Act's beneficial purpose was to enable Aboriginal

---

[105] Shawanaga First Nation, Ontario, Canada (2019). *Court Decision.* Available at: http://shawanagafirstnation.ca/wp-content/uploads/2019/03/RHT-Update.pdf.

[106] *Mason v Tritton* (1994) 34 NSWLR 572, per Kirby P, 584.

[107] See *Walker v New South Wales* (1994) 182 CLR 45, however, this case was distinguishable as it asserted Aboriginal sovereignty. Sir Anthony Mason *rejected* the notion that a limited kind of sovereignty resides in the Aboriginal people as a 'domestic dependent nation' entitled to self-government and not subject to Australian laws until they are adopted, and *rejected* the argument that Aboriginal people are "a free and independent people entitled to any rights and interests, *other than those created or recognised by the laws of the Commonwealth, the State of New South Wales and the common law*". Therefore, this decision is still consistent with the arguments in this paper, that Aboriginal customary law is also entitled to application of the *Mabo* principle—doctrine of *continuity pro tempore* such that it continues and can be recognised as valid by the common law.

[108] *Goodsell v Yunupingu* (1999) *4 Australian Law Reporter* 29, at 37.

people to pursue traditional lives on Aboriginal Land. This implicitly meant the observance and enforcement of traditional laws on that Land. As the Yolngu rights were enforceable under the Act, there was no need to consider whether those rights were also recognised as native title rights at common law.

The Australian common law is, therefore, yet to be fully made and specifically affirmed in a ratio decidendi of the High Court on this point of continuity of Aboriginal law and customs beyond Land-related rights. Indigenous Australian lawyers such as Eddie Cubillo are rightly asking:

> Is it time to take up the challenge of developing the Australian legal system in ways that the court in Mabo [No 2] declined to? To acknowledge Indigenous law and legal authority? Until we do, the flaws in this foundational 'legal fiction' will continue to infect the entirety of Australia's legal system.[109]

Until a constitutional doctrine is established at the Federal level, the States will be free to legislate to refuse to allow Aboriginal laws and customs to be recognised or appropriately considered in matters such as sentencing and bail hearings.[110] Cubillo has also implored Western law-makers to understand that customary law is not an 'historic artefact' as it guides Aboriginal people in fundamental ways in the community on Country and conveys their obligations 'to look after one another and care for country'.[111]

Many Aboriginal Elders have advised our governments of the crucial ingredient that is missing from the Australian justice systems:

> [T]he fundamental importance of reciprocity in the administration of justice: so long as the mainstream legal system disrespects local Aboriginal laws by ignoring them or excluding them, it seems all but inevitable that many Aboriginal Territorians will remain alienated from and disrespectful of mainstream legal authority.[112]

3. Two separate sources of Land title, but native title subject to 'structural inequality'

Wik

In *Wik*,[113] Brennan CJ stated that native title's susceptibility to extinguishment is because 'it is ***not an*** estate held from the Crown nor is it protected by the common law as ***Crown tenures are protected against impairment by subsequent Crown grant***'.[114] For that reason, the extinguishment tests prioritise Crown tenure rights over native title rights.

---

[109] Cubillo (2021), p. 4. Available at: https://journals.sagepub.com/doi/pdf/10.1177/1037969X211019139

[110] See, for example, ss 90 and 91 of the *Northern Territory National Emergency Response Act 2007* (Cth) into ss 15AB and 16AA of the *Crimes Act 1914* (Cth).

[111] Cubillo, op. cit., p. 5.

[112] Northern Territory Law Reform Committee (2020), p. 11.

[113] *The Wik Peoples v The State of Queensland & Ors; The Thayorre People v The State of Queensland & Ors* (1996) 187 CLR 1 ("Wik").

[114] *Wik,* op. cit., per Brennan CJ, [51].

Hepburn argues that this reasoning emphasises the ***'structural inequality*** associated with the implementation of native title within a feudal tenure framework***', which is incapable of achieving equality between non-Indigenous and Indigenous title.***[115]

Given the existing 'Crown control and dependence' native title model, at least the majority decision in *Wik* represented a clear move 'away from the strictures of feudal tenure, revealing an increasing judicial desire to embrace a more balanced and equitable system',[116] to use Hepburn's words.

However, Hepburn's arguments go further in contending that ***Australia should move towards recognising an allodial model*** which confers a more absolute and independent ownership where the native title owner is not subject to the control of a higher authority, but which would have the same ownership status as other common law and statutory interest because it still endures as a burden or encumbrance on the Crown's radical title.[117] Hepburn argues that the difference in the allodial model is purely structural, so it does not create any change in the character of individual ownership rights,[118] and like any form of ownership, is subject to the limitations and rules of the law. However, under this model, ***native title would not be as susceptible to extinguishment as the status of the Crown's title would no longer determine its existence.***[119]

Hepburn's rationale is succinctly stated:

> *Native title has been too important to the development and dissemination of indigenous culture within Australia to be removed. The most appropriate and viable solution for a structured and equalised development of indigenous and non-indigenous title is to abolish feudal tenure. ...There are no enduring legal impediments to the removal of the doctrine of tenure, and ultimately its removal is* ***essential for the creation of a responsive bicultural Land system.***[120]

I agree that an allodial model is one to aspire towards implementing for the reasons Hepburn identifies, including that it would achieve Kirby J's stated objectives in *Wik* that 'ordinary common law principles for the protection of a proprietary right' should apply to Indigenous owners 'in exactly the same way as the law would protect other Australians'.[121]

Arguably, this may mean that the Australian government has an obligation under international law to move the native title model in this direction, given that the *Native Title Act 1993* is legislated as a 'special measure' under s51 (xxvi) of the Constitution,

---

[115] Hepburn, op. cit., p. 27.

[116] Ibid., p. 30.

[117] Ibid., pp. 31–32.

[118] Ibid., p. 32, citing Edgeworth (1994).

[119] Hepburn, op. cit., p. 32, citing Buck (1995).

[120] Ibid., p. 33.

[121] Ibid., p. 36, citing Kirby J in *Wik*, [575].

the 'race power'[122] for the purposes of Article 1(4) of the International Convention on the Elimination of All Forms of Racial Discrimination (ICERD). Article 1(4) of the ICERD states:

> *4.* ***Special measures*** *taken for the sole purpose of securing* ***adequate advancement*** *of certain racial or ethnic groups or individuals requiring such protection as may be necessary in order to* ***ensure such groups or individuals equal enjoyment or exercise of human rights and fundamental freedoms*** *shall* ***not be deemed racial discrimination, provided, however, that such measures do not, as a consequence, lead to the maintenance of separate rights for different racial groups*** *and that they shall not be continued after the objectives for which they were taken have been achieved.*[123]

Under the existing model—one of native title that is subject to the control of the Crown and dependent upon the Crown title's status—common law principles do not apply equally to native title as they do to title derived from Crown tenure. As such, it follows logically that we indeed have a plural Land title system in Australia. More importantly, it follows logically and strategically that the body of law to which those adversely affected must defer for recourse and justice is that of Equity, not the very body of law (common law and statutory law) that entrenches that inequity.

Equity, above all other bodies of law, has the inherent potential to provide the antidote to this classic structural inequity. After all, Equity is a specialist in intervening to remedy injustice in structures where there is special vulnerability due to the imbalance of power created where legal title is held by someone other than its beneficial owner. It is known as the law of fiduciary duties and equitable obligations.

4. First Law rights and interests can be enforced in equity

The fact that First Law is enforceable in Equity, on an equal footing with Crown tenure rights, is an important way in which First Law can be seen as plural with the Australian Western law system:

- Both common law and equitable actions and remedies may apply for proprietary interests in Land, including native title. The latter may include breach of fiduciary duty, breach of trust, breach of other equitable obligations, breach of public duty to administer the law equitably (judicial review), unjust enrichment and restitution;
- Both monetary remedies (e.g. compensation for value) and 'in specie' remedies (e.g. specific rights held on constructive trust) may be available for proprietary native title holders in respect of loss or damage or wrongful dispossession/deprivation of legal rights;
- Native title rights are increasingly being held to exist, on the basis they have not been extinguished by legislation (viewed as regulation, not prohibition), nor

[122] See National Native Title Tribunal (Cth): http://www.nntt.gov.au/Documents/Native%20title%20becomes%20law.pdf#:~:text=Native%20Title%20Act%201993%28Cth%29%2C%20Preamble%202%20%E2%94%82%20Native,protection%20of%2C%20Aboriginal%20Peoples%20and%20Torres%20Strait%20Islanders.

[123] Australian Human Rights Commission. *Federal Discrimination Law: Chapter 3—The Race Discrimination Act.* Available at: https://humanrights.gov.au/our-work/legal/federal-discrimination-law-chapter-3-race-discrimination-act#3_3_1.

extinguished by grants of rights of non-exclusive possession, such as a pastoral lease;
- Native title rights are increasingly being held to comprise commercial use rights, as both regulatory legislation and the NTA (s211) in fact confirm and serve to protect the existence of native title rights. They do not impose a prohibition upon the exercise of those rights.

In determining the nature and content of native title rights, the High Court has held that it is erroneous to focus upon the activity and the purpose, rather than focusing on the relevant native title right, e.g. the right to take fish. Shifting the focus, from *right* to *activity* leads to incorrectly inferentially reframing the question determinative of extinguishment.[124] This form of 'adverse dominion' test was rejected by the High Court in *Ward*.[125]

Extinguishment is not to be determined by concluding that the relevant native title right no longer includes the right to pursue a form of activity, merely because the Crown has asserted control or dominion over the particular activity so as to regulate it.

Proprietary rights such as those derived from traditional laws and custom recognised by the common law (native title) are not, unlike public rights, easily or necessarily freely amenable to abrogation or regulation by a competent legislature.[126] Rather the inconsistency test must be applied, and to the extent rights can co-exist, native title rights will not be extinguished.[127]

In 1994, Sir Anthony Mason remarked that:

> *The ecclesiastical natural law foundations of equity, its concern with standards of conscience, fairness, equality and its protection of relationships of trust and confidence, as well as its discretionary approach to the grant of relief, stand in marked contrast to the more rigid formulae applied by the common law and equip it better to meet the needs of the type of liberal democratic society which has evolved in the twentieth century.*[128]

We must both aspire and act, by arguing legal and equitable claims, to advance the interests of Indigenous peoples under their customary title if we are to bring that vision into reality in the context of First Law.

The High Court in *Ward* endorsed an important statement from *Mabo (No.2)* regarding the protection of native title, namely that native title 'may be protected by such legal or equitable remedies as are appropriate to the particular rights and interests established by the evidence'.[129] Their Honours noted that this is yet to be

---

[124] *Akiba on behalf of the Torres Strait Regional Seas Claim Group v Commonwealth* [2013] HCA 33 ("Akiba"), per Hayne, Kiefel and Bell JJ at 30, [66–67].

[125] *Western Australia v Ward* [2002] HCA 28 ("Ward").

[126] *Akiba*, note 76, per French CJ and Crennan J at [38]. See also Morris (2002). Morris notes that the High Court "rejected the Commonwealth's argument that the claimants' native title rights should be regarded as having been subsumed into the public rights to fish and navigate".

[127] *Western Australia v Brown* [2014] HCA 8 ("Brown").

[128] Mason (1994), p. 239.

[129] *Ward*, op. cit., [21], citing *Mabo (No. 2)*, [113].

developed in the jurisprudence to fully appreciate what the 'appropriate' remedies may be.[130]

In *Mabo (No. 2)*, Deane and Gaudron JJ issued a resounding reminder of the valuable prior rights that subsist in native title Lands, which equitable remedies can protect.[131] Their Honours stated that 'the rights of occupation or use under common law native title can themselves constitute valuable property. ***Actual or threatened interference with their enjoyment can, in appropriate circumstances, attract the protection of equitable remedies', including injunction***.[132] Importantly, their Honours emphasised the common law principle that '*pre-existing native title rights are respected and protected' will prevail over other equitable principles*, just as it prevailed over other legal rules, when native title was recognised by the common law as surviving British sovereignty.[133]

In *Fejo*, the High Court majority discussed the determination-making powers of the NTA, observing that while it establishes a framework for determining native title and recognises and protects it, the NTA 'otherwise does not deal with the ascertainment or enforcement of native title rights *by curial process*' (emphasis added). Accordingly, their Honours said that if a party is seeking to enforce or protect actual or claimed native title rights by way of court order, they 'must take proceedings in a court of competent jurisdiction'.[134] This is confirmation by the High Court of the potential for enforcing native title rights and interests outside of the NTA in order for native title holders to avail themselves of equitable remedies.

These remarks of the High Court in *Mabo (No. 2)* and *Fejo* highlighted above are aligned with my argument that proceedings invoking the equitable jurisdiction are likely to provide greater access to the most suitable and nuanced rules and remedies to effectively enforce and protect native title rights and interests in Australia.[135] Based on all of the 'signals of pluralism' discussed above, I believe that the Australian law has already emerged as *legally plural* and as such, it is ready and ripe (well beyond time) for that plurality to be *fully enforced and implemented*.

---

[130] Ibid.

[131] *Mabo (No. 2)*, op. cit. [113], per Deane and Gaudron JJ, [64]–[65].

[132] Ibid.

[133] Ibid.

[134] *Fejo v Northern Territory of Australia* (1998) 195 CLR 96 ("*Fejo*"), [120–121], [22].

[135] Blowes (1993). Blowes, a Barrister, predicted that the fiduciary issue "is potentially significant—it provides the basis for an array of arguments which may eventually result in softening the implications of the majority finding that subject to the operation of the *Racial Discrimination Act 1975* (Cth), properly authorised extinguishment of traditional title does not give rise to a claim for compensatory damages. If fiduciary obligations become established as a concomitant of traditional title, that association may provide considerable security and protection for traditional title from governmental interference".

4.6 How Can the Nation Help to Create Legal and Institutional Systems that Implement Legal Pluralism to Give Effect to Peace with Nature and Indigenous Peoples?

Australian litigators can be central to our first two goals as part of the transformational shifts that are necessary to implement legal pluralism in Australia. This will involve the following steps, each of which can and should be undertaken *contemporaneously:*

1. Reinstate the Australian Western law's integrity

Resuscitate the Rule of Law—Australian Western law is so far off track from its own institutions that even its own values and core principles are not being upheld. The administration of state laws is being corrupted by system failures that allow private interests to be put before public interest. ***Because the health of the Australian legal system is so central to securing First Law's pluralism*** in the future, and important part of co-design could be to establish a 'Rule of Law' focused program to identify, challenge, create legal precedents for, and eliminate the major factors corrupting the Rule of Law, e.g. political donations paid to major political parties creating a conflict of interest, public funds applied to improper partisan political purposes, and unregulated and unethical commercial media broadcasting, and platforms publishing false and misleading information that is interfering with democracy.

The fundamental human rights of all Australians and the rights of Australia's Indigenous Peoples must be asserted in our environmental protection work. These guaranteed rights give rise to correlative duties of government to take appropriate steps to protect them.[136]

I believe there is no question that human and Indigenous rights are being infringed, and the 'Rule of Law' itself is, therefore, under threat, being entirely compromised by the way in which current Western governments such as Australia are administering the environmental laws. For example, in my view, Federal/State Ministers and other executive decision-makers are or have been unlawfully:

- Granting approvals for new or expanded coal mining projects without due regard to the impact of Scope 3 emissions, thereby not meeting their duty to protect children from climate harm (acknowledging that a duty of care was established by the *Sharma* case[137] but subsequently overturned). However, the *Waratah Coal* case provides a new angle for establishing the existence of such duty, grounded in human rights and ESD mandatory considerations);

[136] Attorney-General's Department. *Right to Life* (Public Sector Guidance Sheet). Available at: https://www.ag.gov.au/rights-and-protections/human-rights-and-anti-discrimination/human-rights-scrutiny/public-sector-guidance-sheets/right-life.

[137] Sharma by her litigation representative Sister Marie Brigid Arthur v Minister for the Environment [2021] FCA 560 ("Sharma").

- Funding new gas-fired power stations and pipeline infrastructure based on advice from a conflict of interest, and contrary to all credible economic,[138] scientific[139] and technological advice[140];
- Excluding renewable energy from the top five priority technologies for reducing emissions in Australia's Nationally Determined Contribution (NDC) submission to the UNFCCC[141] under the Paris Agreement, an unreasonable, capricious and discriminatory policy against renewable energy technologies;
- Proliferating fossil fuels and granting approvals for new gas fracking and extraction projects at this point in history[142] without due regard to mandatory 'Ecologically Sustainable Development' (ESD) considerations of intergenerational equity and the precautionary principle. The ultimate evidence that ESD principles have not been adequately considered and applied is that the approved project infringes human rights, and therefore the approval is in excess of their executive powers (an administrative discretion ends where it intersects with infringing human rights unlawfully);
- Not taking prudential measures such as bonding for future remediation costs e.g. the emerging issue of orphan gas wells becoming 'wards of the state', arguably a breach of their equitable obligations to the public arising from the exercise of their public powers;
- Seeking to mandate that institutional investors and financiers, such as Australian superannuation fund managers and national banks, must invest private money in and finance fossil fuel projects respectively, in breach of their statutory and common law fiduciary duties and duties of care to shareholders and the community in relation to managing and mitigating climate risk.

These decisions are extraordinary and appear to clearly breach the high fiduciary-style obligations and standards that apply in administrative law to public officials, who are exercising public powers that are vested in them by the public trust.[143] In addition, executive decisions are unlawful if they infringe human rights without express authority in clear words, as it is contrary to the principle of legality.[144]

First Nations Peoples could enforce native title rights and interests in Land and waters by invoking the equitable jurisdiction. This might, for example, refer to the program of pastoral lease renewals without consent or consideration that is being executed against WA and NT native title holders. In addition, the expansion of pastoral leases into rangeland leases and other diversified leases (potentially perpetual) in

---

[138] Garnaut (2019).

[139] Climate Targets Panel (2021).

[140] The Climate Council (2021).

[141] United Nations Framework Convention on Climate Change (UNFCCC), Nationally Determined Contributions (NDCs)—Australia, December 2020. Available at: https://www4.unfccc.int/sites/ndcstaging/PublishedDocuments/Australia%20First/Australia%20NDC%20recommunication%20FINAL.PDF.

[142] Estcourt (2021).

[143] French (2010).

[144] Chen (2019).

relation to agricultural activities and new economies such as clean energy generation on Country e.g. commercial solar electricity generation, or green hydrogen production. Where this is being done in favour of pastoralists, and impairing or nullifying native title use and enjoyment and transferring opportunities for sustainable economic development on Country, without consent and often without consideration, it raises the spectre of equitable remedies.[145]

2. Bring First Law to the fore

We need to rectify the major factors leading to the failure to fully enforce and recognise customary law as required by the Australian common law and implement the structural supports necessary to enable such proceedings for the full recognition and enforcement of First Law rights and interests to take place.

First Law comprises its own legally unique (*sui generis*) ontologies, epistemologies and authorities which are part of the First Law normative and governance system. We need to pursue opportunities to seek to have unique native title Songlines and conceptions, such as the Rainbow Serpent, to be rendered in First Law terms. A leading example of this in Australia is the *Warloongarriy* Law (River Law), and the view of the Martuwarra Traditional Custodians that their sacred River is and embodies a living Ancestral being under that Law. This case has the potential to set a precedent in Australia for more such cases to follow, recognising First Law in accordance with its own terms, which in turn could establish authority in the Traditional Custodians to co-manage it under *Wunan* Law (regional governance law).

Under dedicated programs, First Nations and Rights of Nature advocates could establish a First Law-focused program to 'bring First Law to the fore'. This would include identifying, challenging and creating legal precedents and remedies to address the inequities of the current Australian legal system, which could include pursuing the following developments of the law:

- Securing the rendering of native title in customary law terms, as is required by the common law, e.g. Martuwarra Ancestral Being (Rainbow Serpent) is a whole River that is a living ancestor with a right to live and flow, not just a resource of water and separate riverbanks and beds;
- Recognising the prior rights and authorities in relation to the legal and equitable native title rights and interests, e.g. Martuwarra Traditional Owners have shared possession of the River as a whole (as common property), and therefore have co-authority under customary law (native title) to care for the River as a whole living being as that is what they possess, as well as the individual members of the Martuwarra tribes having individual usufructuary rights to use the water and river as a resource;
- Ensuring that both types of Australian proprietary interest in Land are treated and protected equally—there are two sources of Land title in Australia, one from Crown grants and one from pre-existing customary law (First Law), therefore infringement of the rights whether Crown grant Land title, such as a freehold farm,

[145] See Government of Western Australia, Department of Lands, Planning and Heritage, Pastoral Land: https://www.dplh.wa.gov.au/information-and-services/pastoral-land.

or native title should be defended and protected from environmental destruction on an equal, even-handed basis under the environmental law;

- Ensuring that the *sui generis* nature and incidents of native title are protected as property rights and interests, not just protecting the incidents of ordinary Australian property rights—at present the legal system is protecting the physical manifestation of Australian common law property interests e.g. a house, farm and stock, or jewellery, but failing to protect the physical and metaphysical manifestations of many First Law proprietary interests, e.g. Aboriginal heritage such as the ancient Juukan rock shelters,[146] or the Rainbow Serpent and Songlines (River and landscapes), and the Totems (plants and wildlife);
- Holding the Australian government to account for failing to ensure that Native Title Determinations across Australia are updated to reflect the current High Court precedents on the right to use native title Lands for commercial purposes, i.e. specifically granting commercial rights to Crown grant landholders, but not establishing a process to specifically recognise Indigenous native title landholders' commercial use rights in relation to both Lands and waters, as have been recognised by the case law[147]; and
- Holding the governments to account for establishing racially inequitable and discriminatory resource management and regulatory systems, e.g. NSW Water Market barriers and overallocations in the Murray-Darling Basin, which fail to protect or have due regard to pre-existing native title rights and interests.

Australian law, therefore, needs to be brought out of its nightmarish slumber by enforcing the Western 'Rule of Law' and bringing First Law to the fore, before the Australian community sleepwalks into lethal and irreversible ecological disaster with genocidal consequences.[148] Indeed, the world must now take urgent and unprecedented action to heal nature and our climate by re-wilding on a massive scale.[149] First Nations and Rights of Nature advocates have a huge role to play in Australia achieving this goal by bringing First Law to the fore.

---

[146] The AIATSIS submission to the Juukan Gorge destruction inquiry notes that the *Aboriginal Heritage Act WA* (AHA) was created in 1972 and predates both the Native Title Act and Commonwealth heritage legislation. The AHA makes no reference to native title legislation, even though it is common for native title determinations to include a right to protect sites. To date, this protection is not achieved directly though AHA legal processes but via the assertion of cultural connections through heritage protection agreements or ILUAs and maintenance of Country via recognised programs such as the Indigenous Protected Areas program. See https://aiatsis.gov.au/sites/default/files/2021-06/sub-057aiatsispublishedinquiry-destruction-46000-year-old-caves-juukan-gorge.pdf. I, therefore, assert that there is much room for equitable rights and claims to be asserted concurrently/in addition to the native title legislation-based process.

[147] *Akiba*, op. cit.

[148] See United Nations Secretary-General Antonio Guterres' repeated calls for urgent climate policies and science-based targets, in *UN News, Global Perspectives on Human Stories* (2021). World on the verge of climate 'abyss', as temperature rise continues: UN chief. Available at: https://news.un.org/en/story/2021/04/1090072.

[149] Greenfield (2021).

3. Embed a Framework of value-based Principles into policy-making

New Zealand (NZ) offers an excellent example of how the law of a nation state can go some way to being philosophically decolonised through ***formally embedding Māori Indigenous principles and ethics into the policy-making and economic framework***. NZ Government's 'Wellbeing' framework is a framework against which the policies and laws of NZ Treasury such as tax policies, and the economic budgetary decisions are evaluated and assessed.

A 'Wellbeing' Framework for policy-making in Australia, based on the NZ model, has the potential to complement the litigation-based law transformation in goals 1 and 2 above to ensure that our broader legal and economic system values and funds the advancement of all of our forms of capital (Natural, Social, Human and Physical/ Financial), across all of the values we need to serve, across all of the generational time frames. NZ has 12 domains of wellbeing indicators, across three dimensions—people, place and time. These are based on Māori values, ethics and principles. This internalises Indigenous concepts of wellbeing and ethics within state law.

Australia has the opportunity to emulate this approach and embed our own First Peoples' wisdom into an Australian policy-making framework. This is set out in an article I wrote for my fellow tax professionals, expressing the dire need for such a Wellbeing-based framework if we are to achieve a 'green economic recovery' post-COVID-19.[150]

The ***Wellbeing Framework could and should embed Indigenous values and ethics from the law design and development stage.*** Is so, the tax laws and incentives enacted, for example, would likely put a price on carbon emissions and other pollution, and provide subsidies for natural asset conservation regeneration, clean energy and clean transport systems. Environmental law following this evaluation framework would say, for example, that new coal and gas are now *banned* because they are inherently unsustainable, as when the policy is assessed by reference to Indigenous principles such as reciprocity, guardianship, and intergenerational equity, such new developments would be unacceptable.

The Australian government announced that it would explore and consult on developing a Wellbeing Budget for the first time in 2022–23. Overall, stakeholders' feedback supported the government's *Measuring What Matters* framework to monitor advancing progress across a range of wellbeing indicators, beyond GDP. The submissions emphasised the importance of including the experiences of different groups—such as women, First Nations people, veterans, people with disability, and age cohorts, as well as different geographic locations.

---

[150] Bagnall (2020a, 2020b).

The preliminary Framework consists of 12 indicators, across five themes. However, the *Measuring What Matters* paper acknowledges that the whole of population indicators outlined in the Framework are not an accurate measure of First Nations wellbeing as they are limited in their ability to represent these intrinsic cultural differences or acknowledge the past practices that have had detrimental impacts.[151]

The paper notes that the concept of wellbeing for First Nations peoples has always been about 'preserving and maintaining culture, which directly affects mental, physical and spiritual health'. It recognises that 'this is anchored in ways of knowing and being that have existed and continued for tens of thousands of years, shared through complex kinship systems, and passed down through systems of law, lore, ceremony, and song'. Notably, what this is describing is essentially First Law, customs and culture. The paper, therefore, arguably explicitly recognises that the missing ingredient for First Nations' wellbeing to be achieved is the preservation of First Law, customs and culture.

Regrettably, the paper then seems to suggest that the National Agreement on Closing the Gap metrics, and the National Strategic Framework for Aboriginal and Torres Strait Islander Peoples' Mental Health and Social and Emotional Wellbeing (2017–2023) will be the primary means of improving the wellbeing of First Nations people, with the Wellbeing Budget framework supplementing that work.

Instead, the government should have contemplated the notion that the Wellbeing Budget framework could be guided, shaped and enhanced by First Law and cultural principles, values and ethics by embedding them into the fabric of objectives that we measure and monitor, and the tools by which we assess budgetary decisions. The government should consider that Australian wellbeing culture must include and reflect First Nations' wellbeing culture.

After developing a unique Australian framework with Indigenous Elders and Rights of Nature advocates, we will have generated a sound basis for policy and law reform to take forward to Treasury and other relevant government Departments. The discussion that must happen is to convey the need for an economic and fiscal policy evaluation framework that instils ancient Indigenous wellbeing principles and our national values into the 'character' of tax and economic policy architecture. Because our 'character' becomes our destiny.

New Zealand Wellbeing Framework—'He Ara Waiora'

The Aotearoa New Zealand Treasury has developed a framework within its wellbeing model, that can help to understand Māori perspectives on wellbeing.[152] He Ara Waiora is a holistic, intergenerational approach to wellbeing, grounded in wai (water) as the source of ora (life). It articulates both the ends, or what are important

---

[151] Australian Government (2023).

[152] New Zealand Treasury, 'He Ara Waiora', https://protect-au.mimecast.com/s/_mu0Ck81N9tkp7jJXiVA9ke?domain=treasury.govt.nz https://www.treasury.govt.nz/information-and-services/nz-economy/higher-living-standards/he-ara-waiora

elements in Māori perceptions of wellbeing, and the means, or the tikanga principles that help us achieve the ends.

The ends (outcomes/values) are:

- **Wairua** (spirit) is at the centre to reflect that it is the foundation or source of wellbeing. Values, beliefs and practices related to wairua are essential to Māori conceptions of waiora.
- **Te Taiao** (the natural world—the environment) is paramount and inextricably linked with human wellbeing. Humans have responsibilities and obligations to sustain and maintain the wellbeing of Te Taiao.
- **Te Ira Tangata**(the human domain) encapsulates human activities and relationships, including the relationships between generations. The concept of mana (power, authority) is seen as key to wellbeing.

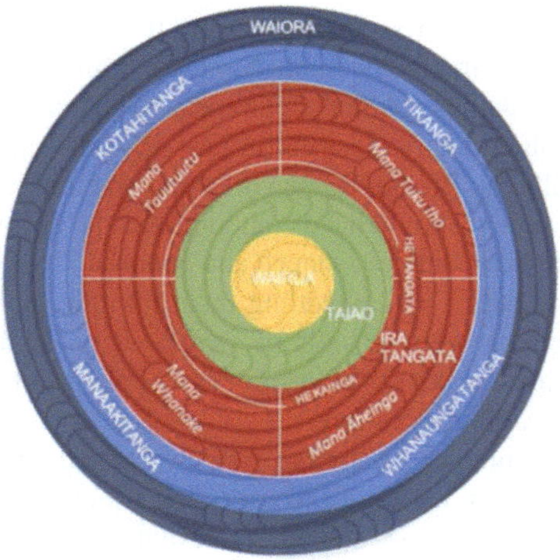

Source New Zealand Treasury

The means, or key principles, are:

- *Kotahitanga*—working in an aligned, coordinated way;
- *Tikanga*—making decisions in accordance with the right values and processes, including in partnership with the Treaty partner;
- *Whanaungatanga*—fostering strong relationships through kinship and/or shared experience that provide a shared sense of wellbeing;
- *Manaakitanga*—enhancing the mana of others through a process of showing proper care and respect;
- *Tiakitanga*—guardianship, stewardship (e.g. of the environment, particular taonga or other important processes and systems).

4.7 Reflections on Key Messages

Using all of our law and thinking holistically

In carrying out the above three steps, we need to use all of our law and all of our knowledge of how our world works. We need to transform our siloed, specialist legal thinking, and think holistically. We need to be inspired by Indigenous peoples' approach to thinking itself and to problem-solving. That is, we need to use connected systems-thinking, just as Indigenous people do when they view the world. We need to see the whole of the legal system, understand the whole of the legal system and draw on our fundamental principles from across our whole legal system. Again, just like First Law, we need to apply the basic principles of our Western law.

As noted, some of the most important components of our Australian legal system appear to have fallen into disuse, but now more than ever they must be called upon and relied upon to both repair and recalibrate the direction of Australian law.

These great 'missing' or waning bodies of law include Equity, jurisprudence[153] and human/Indigenous rights. They should be used in conjunction with our administrative law and constitutional law principles which are foundational to our democracy. We need to get back to first principles in our own law (as well as fully implementing the 'raw law' principles of First Law[154]). We need to be inspired by Eddie Mabo and create new law that recognises or enforces these ancient rights, relationships and authorities.

Wherever it is occurring, we need to have the courage and integrity to assert that the substantive private rights of Australia's Indigenous peoples are being unlawfully infringed and trampled by executive decision-makers if they do not have the legal authority to infringe such rights. These private legal rights are *pre-existing*, they *subsist in our law*, and they *endure* to the extent they have not been extinguished. They are only extinguished where there is a right or interest that is necessarily inconsistent with the customary law in its legal character, not operational inconsistency. Otherwise, native title rights co-exist with Crown grant rights.[155]

Regulatory laws even where prohibitive will only extinguish native title where there are clear and unambiguous words or necessary inconsistency.[156] Potentially, some customary law rights and interests, due to their unique character, may arguably be incapable of extinguishment by inconsistency with common law rights.

To the extent that Australian legislators are purporting to nullify or impair these legal rights or pre-existing equities on unjust terms or under inequitable circumstances, doing so may even lack Constitutional authority, resulting in invalidity. Combined principles of Equity, property, constitutional law principles (including the

---

[153] Hohfeld (1913).

[154] Watson, op. cit.

[155] *Brown,* op. cit. In *Brown* [2014] HCA 8, the High Court confirmed the view that extinguishment is based on the legal nature and content of the rights, not on the manner of use or exercise of the rights.

[156] *Dietman v Karpany* (2012) 112 SASR 514 confirmed that regulation does not affect the ongoing recognition and exercise of native title rights and interests.

Rule of Law), and human rights law, together with native title and the common law may come to bear in determining the legal position.

Indigenous justice and the general Law of Equity go hand in hand

We can expect to find the solutions we are searching for not in any one of these fields of law alone, but at the intersections of, and due to the synergies between, many or all of them. We need to think creatively and innovatively with our legal arguments. As noted above, there is much inspiration, instruction and ammunition to be drawn from a rich and diverse 'quiver' full of High Court judgements, both within Australia and from other jurisdictions. We need to be ambitious in pursuit of Indigenous justice.

However, one body of our law, in my view, is a constant across all fields and therefore has the most potential for achieving economic justice and water justice for Indigenous peoples—that of Equity.

The Hon. Michael Kirby has urged and encouraged the legal profession in these terms:

> *[t]hose Australian lawyers who love equity the most will seek to preserve and adapt the essence of its doctrines. They will listen with respect to scholars who propose new formulations. They will remain open in their minds to deriving new remedies, by analogy, based on equity's history and past creativity... The development of equity's doctrines and remedies by analogy to their essential principles will be restored.*[157]

I wholeheartedly agree with Kirby. Along with his Honour, I also share the dream for a law of Equity that is a 'living contributor to a just and innovative legal system for the Australian people in the present and for all the years to come'.[158]

I see particular potential for Equity to make a 'living contribution' to the enhanced enforcement and enjoyment of native title (and broader customary law) rights and interests due to the unique circumstances, and often appalling treatment and lived experiences of Indigenous Australians which appear to me to engage a raft of doctrines that enliven the equitable jurisdiction.

It is my dream that my own research work will assist Australia's Aboriginal and Torres Strait Islander Peoples to one day soon have their prior rights and pre-existing First Law upheld and enforced according to our country's ultimate law of justice—Equity.

I believe that Equity can and must succeed in 'delivering equity' to Peoples so desperately in need of it, and so incomparably meritorious of it. If ever Equity had a role and a destiny, it is surely to be found here in Australia in rendering long-overdue justice to the world's oldest living culture and custodianship.

Harnessing the power and potential of the ancient maxims of Equity in this context will have the dual benefit of ensuring that both sage and enduring *principles*, and sage and enduring *Peoples from time immemorial* can each continue not only to survive but also to flourish long into the future.

---

[157] Kirby (2008). In the W. A. Lee Equity Lecture delivered at the Queensland University of Technology, Brisbane, 19 November 2008, p. 468.

[158] Ibid., pp. 468–469.

Equity could lead to Allodiality—A superior pluralism

The ultimate utopia would be that equitable outcomes achieved through a concerted, steady and stable program of successfully asserting the principles of Equity to enforce pre-existing customary law rights, in turn create the impetus (or compulsion) for Australia to finally engage with its Indigenous peoples in the outstanding settlement of our national debts.

My vision is it could be the driver that results in the ultimate payoff where Indigenous Australians are placed in a rights-based position of strength so as to secure the Treaties we desperately need to transition our nation to a new model of co-governance of our Lands and waters (Country). That new model is also one which more accurately fits our historical truth—an allodial model. A treaty based on this model would provide a future for all Australian people that is truly free and equal before the law.

The destination medium term may be re-visiting whether a 'Voice' to Parliament, an important aspect of the Uluru Statement from the Heart, can be implemented less formally, given the Referendum for a Constitutional Voice to Parliament devastatingly failed in 2023.[159] The Voice would give effect to Indigenous 'voices' by ensuring that place-based knowledge, ethics, values, First Law, understanding of natural systems, reciprocity and relationships with nature is also fed into and scrutinises Australia's law-making by Federal Parliament in so far as it affects Indigenous Australians.

Ultimately, Australians may also hold a Referendum and register a vote in favour of a Republic which would provide a further opportunity for a wholesale redesign of our Constitution to not only recognise local government and regional governance, but also give full effect to the plural legal system that First Law rights and interests could come to represent in Australia, i.e. an allodial title model. This could form the basis of inverting our current Constitutional governance structure of Federal government down to State, and instead allocate governance authority and powers at the local level and on a regional scale and be entrenched in the new Constitution.

At present, no Australian is truly living in a free country until our First Peoples are unshackled from the perpetual control, vulnerability, inequity and legal straight jacket by which they are restrained. We must all succeed in contributing to the brokering of a just and equitable co-existence that will finally give effect to our illusory anthemic motto—'advance Australia fair'.

If we can succeed in bringing about this pluralistic evolution of Australia's legal system, then over time, we will be able to see our legal pluralism as akin to a weave or a braiding of our two legal systems. The two laws, while separate and distinct, will be inextricably intertwined into one legal, equitable, ethical, ecological and cultural tapestry of which Australia can be proud. The threads of each law will remain intact and true to their own source and identity, but they will mutually reinforce each other through respect and cooperation, living side by side in harmony and prosperity.

We have only to decide our intention and to take the first step towards grasping this opportunity to make our legal pathways truly unified. The Australian legal system

[159] Australian Electoral Commission (2023), https://results.aec.gov.au/29581/Website/ReferendumNationalResults-29581.htm

and Australian citizens as a whole have everything to lose from perpetuating our status quo, and everything to gain from making the Indigenous dream of harmonious legal pluralism our reality.

References

Anker, K., Burdon, P., Carver, G., Maloney, M., & Sbert, C. (2021). *From environmental to ecological law*. Routledge.

Apgar, J. M. (2017). *Biocultural Approaches: Opportunities for Building More Inclusive Environmental Governance*. Institute of Development Studies and Swiss Agency for Development and Cooperation, Working Paper No. 502.

Australian Electoral Commission (2023). https://results.aec.gov.au/29581/Website/ReferendumNationalResults-29581.htm.

Australian Government. (2023). 'Measuring What Matters – Australia's First Wellbeing Framework'. See Box 1 on p.17. Available at: https://treasury.gov.au/publication/p2023-mwm

Bagnall, D. (2020a). Fortescue metals group v Warrie on behalf of the Yindjibarndi People. *Australian Environmental Review, 34*(9&10), 226–231.

Bagnall, D. (2020b). Green economic recovery: The '2020' business case for a 'Wellbeing' Tax Policy framework. *Chartered Accountants Australia and New Zealand*. Available at: https://www.charteredaccountantsanz.com/member-services/technical/tax/tax-in-focus/green-economic-recovery

Bavikatte, K. S., & Bennett, T., (2015). Community stewardship: The foundation of biocultural rights. *Journal of Human Rights and the Environment* 6 (1): 7–29

Bavikatte, K., & Robinson, D. F. (2011). Towards a people's history of the law: biocultural jurisprudence & the nagoya protocol on access and benefit-sharing Law. *Environment and Development Journal, 27*(1), 35–51.

Berry, T. (2002). Rights of the earth: We need a new legal framework which recognises the rights of all living beings. *Resurgence, 214*.

Blowes, R. (1993). *Governments: Can you trust them with your Traditional Title?* Available at: http://www.austlii.edu.au/au/journals/SydLRev/1993/19.pdf

Buck, A. R. (1995). Property law and the origins of Australian egalitarianism. *Australian Journal of Legal History, 145*, 151.

Burdon, P. (2011). The great jurisprudence. In P. Burdon (Ed.), *Exploring wild law: The philosophy of earth jurisprudence*. Wakefield Press.

Burdon, P. (2015). Wild law and the project of earth democracy. In M. Maloney & P. Burdon, *Wild Law in Practice*. Routledge.

Caillon, S., Cullman, G., Verschuuren, B., & Sterling, E. J. (2017). Moving beyond the human–nature dichotomy through biocultural approaches. *Ecology and Society, 22*(4), 27.

Chen, C. W., & Gilmore, M. (2015). Biocultural rights: A new paradigm for protecting natural and cultural resources of Indigenous communities. *Indigenous International Policy Journal, 6*(3).

Chen, B. (2019). The principle of legality: Issues of rationale and application. *Monash University Law Review, 41*(2).

Climate Targets Panel. (2021). *Shifting the burden: Australia's emissions reduction tasks over coming decades*. University of Melbourne. Available at: https://www.climatecollege.unimelb.edu.au/files/site1/docs/%5Bmi7%3Ami7uid%5D/Climate%20Targets%20Panel%20Book%20-%20March%202021.pdf

Collard, S. (2021). Sacred Songlines threatened: WA first nations groups concerned over Andrew Forrest appeal. *NITV News*. Available at: https://www.sbs.com.au/nitv/article/2021/03/29/sacred-songlines-threatened-wa-first-nations-groups-concerned-over-andrew-forrest

Cooper v. Stuart (1889). 14 App Cas, per Lord Watson (51), 291.

Cubillo, E. (2021). 30th Anniversary of the RCIADIC and the 'white noise' of the justice system is loud and clear. *Alternative Law Journal, 0*(0), 1–8.

Dancer, H. (2021). Harmony with Nature: Towards a deep legal pluralism. *The Journal of Legal Pluralism and Unofficial Law, 53*(1), 21–41.

Edgeworth, B. (1994). Tenure, allodialism and indigenous rights at common law: English, United States, and Australian land law compared after *Mabo v Queensland. Anglo-American Law Review, 397*, 402.

Eichlera, J., & Navarro, F. V. M. (2023). Proceduralising indigenous peoples' demands: Indigenous environmental rights and legal pluralism in contemporary jurisprudence. *Legal Pluralism and Critical Social Analysis, 55*(1), 5–34.

Elsana, M. (2019). Legal pluralism and indigenous peoples' rights: Challenges in litigation and recognition of indigenous peoples rights. *University of Cincinnati Law Review, 87*(4), 1043–1076.

Engle Merry, S. (1988). Legal pluralism. *Law & Society Review, 22*(5), 869–896.

French, R. (2010). The Interface between Equitable Principles and Public Law. Speech to the Society of Trust and Estate Practitioners, Sydney, 29 October 2010. Available at: https://cdn.hcourt.gov.au/assets/publications/speeches/current-justices/frenchcj/frenchcj29oct10.pdf

Estcourt, D. (2021). Canberra opens bids for gas, oil drilling near Twelve Apostles. *The Age*. Available at: https://amp-theage-com-au.cdn.ampproject.org/c/s/amp.theage.com.au/national/victoria/canberra-opens-bids-for-gas-oil-drilling-near-twelve-apostles-20210615-p5819t.html

Girard, F., Hall, I., & Frison, C. (Eds.) (2022). *Biocultural rights, indigenous people and local communities: Protecting culture and the environment*. Routledge Earthscan.

Garnaut, R. (2019). Australia could fall apart under climate change, but there is a way to avoid it? *The Conversation*. Available at: https://theconversation.com/australia-could-fall-apart-under-climate-change-but-theres-a-way-to-avoid-it-126341

Goodsell v. Yunupingu (1999). *Australian Indigenous Law Book er, 4*(2), 37.

Gover, K. (2020). Legal pluralism and indigenous legal traditions. In P. Schiff Berman (Ed.), *The Oxford Handbook of global legal pluralism* (pp. 847–881). Oxford University Press.

Graham, N. (2011). Lawscape: Property, environment and law. *Journal of Environmental Law, 160*.

Gray, J. (2002). Is native title a proprietary right? *Murdoch University Electronic Journal of Law, 9*(3).

Greenfield, P. (2021). World must rewild on massive scale to heal nature and climate, UN says. *The Guardian*. Available at: https://amp-theguardian-com.cdn.ampproject.org/c/s/amp.theguardian.com/environment/2021/jun/03/rewild-on-massive-scale-to-heal-nature-and-climate-says-un-decade-on-ecosystem-restoration-aoe

Hepburn, S. (2005). Disinterested truth: Legitimation of the doctrine of tenure post-mabo, *29*(1).

Hohfeld, W. (1913). Some fundamental legal conceptions as applied in Judicial Reasoning. *Yale Law Journal*, 28–59. Available at: http://www.law.harvard.edu/faculty/cdonahue/courses/prop/mat/Hohfeld.pdf

Jonas, W. A. M. (2002). Recognising aboriginal sovereignty—Implications for the treaty process. Presented at ATSIC National Treaty Conference, 27 August 2002. Available at: https://humanrights.gov.au/about/news/speeches/recognising-aboriginal-sovereignty-implications-treaty-process-2002

Kirby, M. (2008). Equity's Australian isolationism. *Queensland University of Technology Law & Justice Journal, 8*(2), 444.

Lynch, J. (2018). *Calls to give legal rights to nature flow to WA's South West*. ABC South West WA. Available at: https://www.abc.net.au/news/2018-03-23/call-to-give-margaret-river-same-legal-rights-as-humans/9578090

Maffi, L. (2005). Linguistic, cultural, and biological diversity. *Annual Review of Anthropology, 34*, 599–617.

Maloney, M. (2018). Changing the legal status of nature: Recent developments and future possibilities. *NSW Law Society Journal, 49*, 78–79.

Marina Agar, J., (2017) *Biocultural approaches: Opportunities for building more inclusive environmental governance*. IDS Working Paper No. 502.

Martuwarra Fitzroy River Council. (2016). Fitzroy River Declaration. Available at: https://d3n8a8pro7vhmx.cloudfront.net/environskimberley/pages/303/attachments/original/1512653115/fitzroy-river-declaration.pdf?1512653115

Martuwarra, RiverOfLife, Poelina, A., McDuffie, M., & Perdrisat, M. (2023). Martuwarra Fitzroy River Watershed: One society, one river law. *PLOS Water 2*(9), at page 9, e0000104. https://doi.org/10.1371/journal.pwat.0000104

Mason, S. A. (1994). The place of equity and equitable remedies in the contemporary common law world. *Law Quarterly Review*, 238–259.

Minister for Treaty of Waitangi Negotiations. (2012). *Whanganui river agreement signed.* Available at: https://www.beehive.govt.nz/release/whanganui-river-agreement-signed

Morris, J. (2002). Sea Country - the Croker Island Case: Commonwealth of Australia v Yarmirr. *Indigenous Law Bulletin, 5*(14), 18.

Northern Territory Law Reform Committee. (2020). *Two justice systems working together: Book on the recognition of local aboriginal laws in sentencing and bail* (Book 46), 9–10.

O'Donnell, E., Poelina, A., Pelizzon, A., & Clark, C. (2020). Stop burying the Lede: The essential role of indigenous law(s) in creating rights of nature. *Transnational Environmental Law*, 1–25

Pelizzon, A., & Ricketts, A. (2015). Beyond Anthropocentrism and Back Again: From Ontological to Normative Anthropocentrism. *The Australasian Journal of Natural Resources Law and Policy, 18*(2), 105–124.

Posey, D. (2002). Upsetting the sacred balance: Can the study of indigenous knowledge reflect cosmic connectedness? In P. Sillitoe, A. Bicker, & J. Pottier (Eds.), *Participating in development: Approaches to indigenous knowledge.* Routledge.

Rohe, J. R., Govan, H., Schlüter, A., & Ferse, S. C. A. (2019). A legal pluralism perspective on coastal fisheries governance in two Pacific Island countries. *Marine Policy, 100*, 90–97.

Sajeva, G. (2015). Rights with limits: Biocultural rights–between self-determination and conservation of the environment. *Journal of Human Rights and the Environment, 6*(1), 30–54.

Sanjay Kabir Bavikatte. (2014). *Stewarding the earth: Rethinking property and the emergence of biocultural rights.* Oxford University Press.

Secher, U. (2005). The Mabo Decision—Preserving the distinction between settled and conquered or ceded territories. *University of Queensland Law Journal, 24*(1), 35–71.

Short, L. (2014). Tradition versus power: When Indigenous customs and state laws conflict. *Chicago Journal of International Law, 15*, 376–408.

Tamanaha, B. Z. (2021). *Legal pluralism explained: History, theory, consequences* (p. 3). Oxford University Press.

Techera, E. J. (2010). Legal pluralism, Indigenous people and small island developing states: Achieving good environmental governance in the South Pacific. *The Journal of Legal Pluralism and Unofficial Law, 42*(61), 171–204.

The Climate Council. (2021). *An appalling decision: Federal government to fund new gas-fired power station.* Available at: https://www.climatecouncil.org.au/resources/appalling-decision-federal-government-fund-new-gas-power-station/

Tribunal, W. (1999). *Whanganui River Book, Case WAI167, New Zealand.* Available at: https://forms.justice.govt.nz/search/Documents/WT/wt_DOC_68450539/Whanganui%20River%20Book%201999.pdf

Union of Sovereign First Nations of the Northern Murray-Darling Basin. (2017). *Treaty.* Available at: https://nban.org.au/index.php/treaty/#:~:text=Union%20of%20Sovereign%20First%20Nations,Nation's%20own%20Laws%20and%20Customs

von Benda-Beckmann, F. (2002). Who's afraid of legal pluralism? *Journal of Legal Pluralism & Unofficial Law, 47*, 37.

von Benda-Beckmann, K., & Turner, B. (2018). Legal pluralism, social theory, and the state. *The Journal of Legal Pluralism and Unofficial Law, 50*(3), 255–274.

Wainwright, S. (2017). *Murray darling nations sign treaty, hoping for a stronger voice on Indigenous rights.* ABC Broken Hill. Available at: https://www.abc.net.au/news/2017-05-11/murray-darling-aboriginal-nations-sign-treaty/8518228

Chapter 5
Conclusion

This book has been a journey into seeking or making connections, and (re) connections, between Indigenous, and 'non-Indigenous' legal systems, and between these and Earth Law. In doing this, the book provides particular space for the many voices that must be heard and listened to, in establishing those connections, through an Indigenous Think Tank of First Nations and Pacific Islander experts who share their unique wisdom as co-authors.

The journey is one of healing; of repair. We are calling it a *Declaration of Peace for Indigenous Peoples and Nature* because that can signify a journey of connecting, and of repair and healing that must be done if we are to live together in wellbeing in an increasingly fragmented and troubled world. Amidst the ravages of the Anthropocene, the human-induced climate crisis, and a post-COVID-19 world, comes an urgent call for unity and collaboration, to work together to build equitable and just systems of law, of policy and of practice. This book has called attention to the need to bring Indigenous knowledges, stories and First Laws together in harmony with 'Western' systems in plurality, to work together in fashioning new forms of 'pluriverse', or of 'multivocality', embracing a full recognition of Indigenous First Law.

This *Declaration of Peace* explores the potential for developing forms of legal pluralism and approaches to Indigenous ecological, biocultural governance, in what we hope may contribute towards a healing from the legacies, histories and traumas of colonial dispossession and the resulting devastating losses to First Nations laws, languages and cultures. The colonial legacy has also resulted in loss, damage and destruction of Indigenous heritage, including the heritage vested in biological diversity, in ecologies and environments and the knowledge associated with these. The legacies of the theft and destruction of Indigenous knowledges, of epistemologies—in what may be referred to as epistemicide—are also deeply etched and scarred within the traumas of colonial loss.

To this end, we have brought together seven Indigenous voices as the Indigenous Think Tank, sharing their stories, some personal and candid, others of a more

A. Poelina et al., *Declaration of Peace for Indigenous Australians and Nature*,
https://doi.org/10.1007/978-981-99-9327-7_5

academic tone but still coming from the distinct perspectives of Australian First Nations and of Pacific Islander people. These voices and stories, in concert with those of the three non-Indigenous authors, tell the story of connections.

Declaration of Peace then examines possibilities for fashioning new forms of plural legalism and Indigenous bio-governance in the hope that these may offer pathways towards more just futures.

Correction to: Introduction

Correction to:
Chapter 1 in: A. Poelina et al., *Declaration of Peace for Indigenous Australians and Nature*, https://doi.org/10.1007/978-981-99-9327-7_1

The original version of the book was inadvertently published with repeated text in Section 1.2.2 of Chapter 1 which has now been corrected. The book and the chapter have been updated with these changes.

The updated version of this chapter can be found at
https://doi.org/10.1007/978-981-99-9327-7_1

A. Poelina et al., *Declaration of Peace for Indigenous Australians and Nature*,
https://doi.org/10.1007/978-981-99-9327-7_6

Postface

Greg Campbell

Author, *Total Reset* (2022)

This *Declaration of Peace for Indigenous Peoples and Nature* is a call for humanity to cease warring against them, not only because of the injustice and destruction wrought, but also because our wellbeing is inextricably linked with that of the natural world and the application of the knowledge possessed by Indigenous peoples about our Whole Earth system and sapiens' role in its wellbeing and stability.

The First Peoples of Australia have long recognised that the self-regulating, balanced functioning of our planet and its diverse forms and phenomena are a consequence of all elements of the system abiding by their respective operating principles. It is part of the architecture of the First Law. As the First Peoples know, every species has its Law and originally, every society.

The concept of 'Earth Law' can be traced (though not explicitly articulated as such) in part through the writings of individuals such as legal scholar Christopher Stone, whose 1972 book *Should Trees Have Standing* has been an important influence, and Thomas Berry, whose *The Great Work* (1999) is another seminal text. The concept has resonated far and wide, with New Zealand becoming the first nation to legislate recognition of an entire ecosystem (the Whanganui River, including its non-material aspect) as a legal person with no fewer rights than any other person.

Advocates of Earth Law acknowledge the Universe as the primary lawgiver, accept that there is a relational-based existence between people and the broader Earth Community, and affirm all have rights to exist and contribute to our planet's wellbeing. It is soundly based, and with much potential but is a mere fifty years old.

First Law is ancient and timeless. It has been operating from Day One, providing ever-reliable guidance for an ecologically healthy planet devoid of wars of conquest and control and with people leading empowered dignified lives of relative abundance and inner riches. It is First Law that protects our planet, not human laws unless they align with it. As Anne Poelina says, "the Law is in the land, not in man".

A. Poelina et al., *Declaration of Peace for Indigenous Australians and Nature*, https://doi.org/10.1007/978-981-99-9327-7

One day while sitting in a bush camp chatting about Country with Lulu, an elderly Nykina man and widely respected Law-Keeper of High Degree (during the first decade of our work on the recently published book, *Total Reset*[1]), he said, "Law always been here, always will. He not goin', anywhere. He here right now. We sittin' on 'im. Yair, Law is in Country, Country is in Law".

Directly experiencing that fact means connecting with Country, full stop. Knowing First Law means knowing how to walk in the field of a more subtle awareness—observing, listening, seeing and feeling from the still depths of simply being. When the button of intuitive awareness is permanently on and we are connected, our understanding is transformed and our life. It is not without reason the authors refer to Goethe's view that the way to understand things is "through prolonged emphatic looking and seeing grounded in direct experience".

I have never met another human being who does not want an equitably managed, peaceful, abundant and enduring world. But that is only possible if our politico-socioeconomic structures and systems operate in alignment with First Law. Today, they do not and the consequences are plain to see: climate and ecological crises, rampant species extinction, endless geo-political conflicts, expanding inequalities, rising rates of mental illness and so on.

First Law, emanating from the non-material dimension of reality (generally known by the First Peoples as the Dreaming), illumines the place and purpose of every species, each with its unique blueprint for living as an interconnected part of the whole. It encodes an account of the true nature of reality and of the way of things as well as the principles for each species to survive and flourish in a continuing dance of life.

The automatic consequence of people living in alignment with the First Law is a balanced system, homeostasis. It is the permanent cure for the world's illnesses and why people's awareness of the First Law and associated rights and obligations is crucial to humanity's future. It is what enables our species to diligently perform its function. As Lulu emphasised whenever I asked him about humanity's role on our planet, **"The job of humans is to keep the balance of all life"**. It is why our species is endowed with its distinctive capabilities and why it is about 'we' not 'me' as this paper's authors assert.

The authors' advocacy for the elevation of First Law as a crucial platform for the continuance of our species is prescient. As First Law has always existed it does not need to be discovered or created, only to be recognised and re-positioned as the fulcrum of society.

The easiest starting point for reactivating First Law is to listen to the voices of those who have carried it intact from Day One, the First Peoples of Australia. How else could their societies have endured for 65,000 + years? It is why people involved in policy development and decision-making today need to pay close attention to the themes of this substantive paper.

[1] Campbell (2022).

As its title suggests, one pathway for Australia's return to First Law is the implementation of existing jurisprudential recognition of both ancient and modern law—legal pluralism. By progressively weaving together First Law and human-made law, the two can be "inextricably intertwined into one legal, equitable, ethical, ecological and cultural tapestry of which Australia can be proud" (Bagnall, above). In effect, "the embryonic form of an intact, collective spiritual identity for all Australians, which will inform and support our daily, safe lives, our legal and political systems, aspirations and creative genius" (Graham, above).

It is a powerful idea, typifying the Indigenous ethos of respect and cooperative endeavour. If, as Donna Bagnall suggests, the law of equity, which has long existed to correct unjust outcomes under the common law, is re-invigorated it could act as a practical bridging mechanism. Her essay, *Legal Pluralism—An analysis of the current law and future possibilities* in this book, is compelling reading, a springboard for anyone in the legal profession to make their mark on the progressive evolution of the law of the land.

Another strategy the authors advance is the integration of the two laws, "privileging Indigenous First Laws separate, but complementary to Western law" (above). Some may feel that is a little ambitious but the state of the world is now so patently degraded and increasingly unstable that a refusal to countenance a wide range of sensible politico-socioeconomic strategies for returning things to balance constitutes complicity in our world's demise.

More important than human and financial capital firing up technological innovation is the need for it to ignite politico-socioeconomic innovation. As the land of a living First Law, Australia is in the box seat to lead the world. There is no objective reason why any one or more of its 89 bioregions and 419 sub-regions should not see the privileging of First Law where it is still held by the First Peoples. Logically, that means a regional governance framework informed by First Law which holds autonomous, place-based, eco-centric and kin-centric egalitarian human societies as central to the web of life. They are commonly known as holistic societies.

The societal structure for Australia was never centralised governance with a few states and territories; it was regional, place-based self-governance for the benefit of its human and non-human inhabitants and their ecosystem or bio-region. The widely noted superb condition of the continent of Australia in 1788 is proof it was astutely managed by its web of hundreds of interconnected holistic societies.

As governance was decentralised, the linking mechanisms were sophisticated. There was the Law-anchored ethos of mutual respect, of caring and sharing and giving rather than taking with long-standing systems and protocols to facilitate the dynamics of cooperative interdependency and collaboration. One example is the immensely powerful, highly significant songline system that connects the entire continent. It is always resonating. Lulu would have wholeheartedly agreed with Mary Graham's statement, "The concept and practice of Regenerative Songlines is one of the best ways of strengthening and maintaining the Law …" (above).

The re-emergence of the Indigenous relationalities-based holistic model as a dominant feature of society is crucial to the future of life on this planet. Tyson Yunkaporta bluntly warns that if First Law does not prevail, a cataclysm awaits us. But he also books the good news that First Law is accessible to everybody and "has the capacity to engage all people in the vital work of creating regenerative systems in every area of human endeavour" (above).

The stories, insights and recommendations presented by the authors flow not from ideological perspectives or narrow self-interest but from a deep wellspring of traditional wisdom and the classically high ethical Indigenous standard of respect for the sanctity and wellbeing of all life. These are writings worthy of close study and contemplation for they contain the power to inspire the kinds of initiatives so desperately needed.

Humanity can no longer afford to indulge in more decades of profligacy and destruction. As Anne Poelina writes, "we are in a moment in time to right-size the planet and rebalance energy systems through a pluriverse of brave human beings who are coming together to dream a new way of living and being" (above).

There is a lot of work to do together, the whole human family (powerbrokers and billionaires included). It might be very challenging but it is hard to imagine any endeavour more worthy than working for the present and future wellbeing of all life.

Reference

Campbell, G. (2022). *Total reset: Realigning with our timeless holistic blueprint for living*. Total Reset. https://totalreset.com.au/

A. Poelina et al., *Declaration of Peace for Indigenous Australians and Nature*,
https://doi.org/10.1007/978-981-99-9327-7

MIX
Papier aus verantwortungsvollen Quellen
Paper from responsible sources
FSC® C105338

If you have any concerns about our products,
you can contact us on
ProductSafety@springernature.com

In case Publisher is established outside the EU,
the EU authorized representative is:
Springer Nature Customer Service Center GmbH
Europaplatz 3, 69115 Heidelberg, Germany

Printed by Libri Plureos GmbH
in Hamburg, Germany